Marieluise Beck (ed.)

Understanding Ukraine

Tracing the Roots of Terror and Violence

With a foreword by Dmytro Kuleba

UKRAINIAN VOICES

Collected by Andreas Umland

The book series "Ukrainian Voices" publishes English- and German-language monographs, edited volumes, document collections, and anthologies of articles authored and composed by Ukrainian politicians, intellectuals, activists, officials, researchers, and diplomats. The series' aim is to introduce Western and other audiences to Ukrainian explorations, deliberations and interpretations of historic and current, domestic, and international affairs. The purpose of these books is to make non-Ukrainian readers familiar with how some prominent Ukrainians approach, view and assess their country's development and position in the world. The series was founded, and the volumes are collected by Andreas Umland, Dr. phil. (FU Berlin), Ph. D. (Cambridge), Associate Professor of Politics at the Kyiv-Mohyla Academy and an Analyst in the Stockholm Centre for Eastern European Studies at the Swedish Institute of International Affairs.

Marieluise Beck (ed.)

UNDERSTANDING UKRAINE

Tracing the Roots of Terror and Violence

With a foreword by Dmytro Kuleba

ibidem
Verlag

Bibliographic information published by the Deutsche Nationalbibliothek
Die Deutsche Nationalbibliothek lists this publication in the Deutsche Nationalbibliografie; detailed bibliographic data are available in the Internet at http://dnb.d-nb.de.

Bibliografische Information der Deutschen Nationalbibliothek
Die Deutsche Nationalbibliothek verzeichnet diese Publikation in der Deutschen Nationalbibliografie; detaillierte bibliografische Daten sind im Internet über http://dnb.d-nb.de abrufbar.

Editor: Marieluise Beck
Zentrum für die Liberale Moderne gGmbH
Reinhardtstr. 15
10117 Berlin
Telefon +49 (0)30 - 25 09 58 70
info@libmod.de
www.libmod.de

www.ukraineverstehen.de

Editorial work: Julia Eichhofer, Saskia Heller
Academic consulting: Valeriya Golovian, Mattia Nelles
Copy-editing: Academic Consulting Services, Oxford

Illustrations: Hannah Brückner

Typesetting: Jana Dävers, *ibidem* Press

Contribution by Anne Applebaum:
Preface from RED FAMINE: STALIN'S WAR ON UKRAINE by Anne Applebaum
copyright © 2017 by Anne Applebaum.
Used by permission of Doubleday, an imprint of the Knopf Doubleday Publishing Group, a division of Penguin Random House LLC. All rights reserved.

ISBN-13: 978-3-8382-1773-4
© *ibidem*-Verlag, Stuttgart 2023
All rights reserved.

Printed in the United States of America

Contents

Chapter 2: Occupation Forces in the Second World War

Chapter 3: Remembrance and Responsibility

Preface to the New Edition April 2022

Marieluise Beck

We are creating a new edition of the book. On February 24, 2022, the Russian Federation invaded Ukraine under the completely absurd pretext that it had to protect the Russian population in the Donbas. Putin stated the "denazification" and demilitarization of Ukraine as the war's goal. This is a cynical euphemism for the destruction of Ukraine's national independence. For months, the Russian military had encircled Ukraine watched by world public opinion. However, the West would not believe the warnings that Putin was serious.

The Ukrainian president's almost pleading requests to equip Ukraine militarily so it could withstand an attack have been met hesitantly. This creates the feeling of being left alone in Ukraine.

In this sense, the historical review of this booklet is extremely helpful.

The experience of the Holodomor has entered the DNA of the Ukrainian nation. So have the Soviet occupation and the terror under Stalin. Friendly recommendations that Ukraine submits to Putin's demands and remains neutral — and thus unprotected — are blind to history.

For Germans, it is necessary to realize the scale of the immense campaign of extermination that the Wehrmacht, SS and police battalions wrought, especially on the soil of Ukraine. If this Germany does not now stand by Ukraine and give the Ukrainians all the support they need to defend their freedom, it will cause great disappointment and bitterness.

This war is not taking place in a history-free space. Anyone who wants to understand the Ukrainians and their struggle for freedom and self-determination will better understand what is at stake after reading this volume.

Berlin, March 2022

9

Preface

Marieluise Beck

We want to go to Europe! This call of the Maidan was one of the most powerful driving forces of the democratic awakening in Ukraine. Europe stood for democracy, the rule of law, freedom of travel and a better life. Historically, geographically and culturally, Ukraine belongs to Europe. This fact was forgotten after the division of Europe in Yalta. This division into East and West, which Roosevelt, Churchill and Stalin sealed in the Crimea, lasted over half a century. Thus, our common history was forgotten. Forgotten were the old affiliations, the old names, languages were suppressed and the knowledge of geographical coordinates.

With the Iron Curtain, the national self-determination of Eastern Europe was also lost. Attempts to shake off the Soviet empire were bloodily put down in Budapest, Prague and Warsaw.

Following the establishment of the European Economic Community and eventually the European Union, a European community limited to the West emerged. The people in the East were increasingly lost from sight. People were ready to come to terms with the division of Europe. It was forgotten that Central Eastern Europe was multicultural, that the Memel was considered a Jewish river, that there was once a powerful Lithuanian-Polish kingdom, that the Hanseatic League stretched from Lübeck to Riga, that the nobility in St. Petersburg spoke French, that Odesa was a place of Italian master builders, gifted musicians and German piano makers. It was also forgotten that Armenia, like Georgia, saw itself as part of Christian Europe.

The fall of the Iron Curtain gave us the unexpected opportunity to rediscover this Europe as a whole. We encounter the forgotten and the repressed, the misuse and distortion of historical facts, and many taboos. We meet peoples long denied appearing on the map as independent nations and whose languages were systematically suppressed in favor of Russian. Monstrous acts of violence associated with the name of Stalin drove millions of people to their deaths through starvation, forced labor, and shootings. With inconceivable crimes, the SS and Wehrmacht systematically exterminated the Jewish population and treated the Slavs as "subhumans." Timothy Snyder has called the stretch of land from the Baltic Sea to the Black Sea the "Bloodlands" — the earth there is soaked in blood.

The powerful call for freedom and the end of the corrupt rule of the few over the many, for the end of arbitrariness and violence, was the Maidan of 2013/14, which put Ukraine back on the cognitive map of Europe. Nearly seventy years under the umbrella of the Soviet Union made the country almost invisible.

Deeply burned into Ukrainian DNA is the experience of the Holodomor: starvation by the millions in the land of fertile black earth, starvation, especially in the countryside, where even the seeds were confiscated. We do not know exactly how many millions fell victim to this deliberately brought about mass death. The fact that Stalin had the intelligentsia and the Ukrainian cadres of the Communist Party murdered in addition to the peasants' points to all the characteristics of systematic genocide. Those who do not know this history may ask why most Ukrainians so vehemently reject Moscow's supposed protection. They have a keen sense that the masters of the Kremlin are striving to restore the Russian Empire. An independent, sovereign Ukraine stands in the way of these ambitions.

The imperial mania of Hitler's Germany hit the "Bloodlands" particularly cruelly. World War II began in the West with the invasion of Poland by the German Wehrmacht on September 1, 1939. Just 17 days later, Stalin's Red Army joined them from the East. Stalin and Hitler had concluded a devil's pact, the implementation of which destroyed Poland and made Galicia the site of cruel nationalist excesses. Among the followers of Ukrainian nationalist Stepan Bandera, the German attack on the Soviet Union created the devastating illusion that the Germans would free them from the Soviet yoke.

Unimaginable crimes against the Slavic population were committed by the German Wehrmacht. Germans should know Koriukivka, where the Wehrmacht murdered almost 7000 civilians in two days in retaliation for partisan attacks. Adolf Hitler offered Transnistria, Bukovina and southern Ukraine to Romanian dictator Ion Antonescu as a reward for his cronyism. Thus, they murdered together. Romanian troops wiped out the Jewish population in Chernivtsi. German troops stood outside Odesa and left the killing to their Romanian allies. In October 1941, at least 25,000 Jews were burned to death in military barracks where they had been herded beforehand. The dimension of this crime is reminiscent of Babyn Yar.

Hundreds of thousands of Jews were deported to ghettos in Transnistria, where they perished miserably. In Ukraine, according to Yahad-In Unum, there were 2000 execution sites where SS, police battalions, soldiers of the Wehrmacht and local auxiliary police murdered mainly Jewish people. Slav partisans and French prisoners of war were also among the victims. The "Shoah by bullets" preceded industrial extermination camps such as Auschwitz.

This history of double tyranny by the two imperial superpowers, the Soviet Union and the Third Reich, gives rise in Ukraine, as in other Eastern European countries, to a deep-seated unease with Berlin when it concludes treaties at the expense of third parties, as it once did with Moscow.

It is time to face this history. Its long lines continue to have an effect. It will only lose its destructive power if the historical experiences, the violence experienced and the traumatic experiences of the peoples of Central and Eastern Europe are brought to the fore. Only the truth makes reconciliation possible.

We thank all those who made it possible for us to rediscover the forgotten and thus also to understand our history anew. Germany, Ukraine and 47 other countries: together, we are Europe. My special thanks go to the authors of this book and the editorial team of the Zentrum Liberale Moderne, especially Saskia Heller, Julia Eichhofer, Valeriya Golovina and Mattia Nelles.

Foreword

Dmytro Kuleba

Germany and Europe as a whole have come a long way since the first edition of this book in terms of truly understanding Ukraine. Furthermore, precisely this understanding proved to be the key to fully comprehending both Russia's imperial genocidal war of choice and Ukraine's steadfast determination to fight until victory.

I am confident that in the coming years, Ukrainian studies will be introduced at major European universities — not as a replacement for Russian studies, but as an essential component of European studies. Without understanding Ukraine, it proved impossible to comprehend what Europe is now and what it will be in the future.

The essays in this book provide insightful looks into the psychological traumas — mostly terror traumas — survived by Ukrainians throughout the twentieth century. At the same time, it can and should be interpreted as the story of Ukrainian resistance and the people of Ukraine learning to resist. Ukraine's path to healing itself and achieving independence.

Since last year, Germany and Europe as a whole have proven to be our true allies in defending our shared values, freedom, and democracy. But Ukraine has a lot of respect and gratitude for more than just this.

Given our bloody history, many generations of Europeans have been raised in a pacifist spirit. However, Russian aggression has made us all rethink pacifism. True pacifism entails actively defending peace rather than making abstract calls for it. And certainly not by leaving those who defend liberty defenseless in the face of a maniacal dictator attempting to drown Europe in blood.

Europe and Germany have shown they are willing to change their perspectives and adapt to the new reality.

Empathetic desire to comprehend Ukraine has changed the decades-long unfair view of our country through the crooked Russian lens. In November 2022, the German Bundestag made the historic decision to recognize the Holodomor of 1932-1933 as genocide. In Germany's and Europe's view of Ukraine, this marked another watershed, a Zeitenwende-momentum.

I appreciate this book's authors, editors, and publishers. I am grateful to each and every reader for their interest. I hope my third foreword will be dedicated to a peaceful Europe after Ukraine's victory.

Introduction

Timothy Snyder

Why should we be discussing historical responsibility just now, why, when a whole series of elections between populists and others is being carried out across Europe, why, when the Constitutional system of the USA is under threat from within, why, when Russia has invaded and occupied a part of Ukraine, why in this moment should we talk about historical responsibility?

My answer is that it is precisely for those reasons that one must talk about historical responsibility. There are many causes of the problems within the European Union and there are many causes for the crisis of the rule of law in the United States, but one of them is precisely the inability to deal with certain aspects of history.

Let me begin talking about Germany by talking about the United States. Why do we have the government that we have now? How can we have a president of the United States in 2017 who is irresponsible on racial issues? How can we have an Attorney General in 2017 who is a white supremacist? Because we have failed to deal with important questions of our own past, failed to take historical responsibility for certain important parts of our history.

The President wonders aloud why we fought a civil war, why it was after all that there had to be a conflict in America about slavery.

The question of slavery, precisely the question of what a colony is like, of what an empire is like, leads us directly to what I take to be the blind spot in German historical memory.

Ukraine as a centre of Hitler's ideology

The American frontier empire was built largely by slave labor. It was precisely that model of frontier colonialism that was admired by Adolf Hitler. And it was a question for Hitler: who will the racial inferiors be? Who will the slaves be in the German Eastern empire?

And the answer that he gave in theory in *Mein Kampf*, and in practice in the invasion of 1941, the answer was: *the Ukrainians.*

The Ukrainians were to be at the center of a project of colonization and enslavement. They were to be treated as *Afrikaner*, as *Neger* as German documents from the war show. By analogy with the United States, the idea was to create a slavery-driven, exterminatory regime in Eastern Europe with the center in Ukraine.

The purpose of the Second World War, from Hitler's point of view, was the conquest of Ukraine. It is therefore senseless to commemorate any part of the Second World War without beginning from Ukraine. Any commemoration of WWII which involves the Nazi purposes, the ideological, economic, and political purposes of the Nazi regime, must begin precisely from Ukraine.

German policies all focus precisely on Ukraine: The Hunger Plan, with its notion that tens of millions of people were going to starve in the winter of 1941; the Generalplan Ost, with its idea that millions of more people will be forcibly transported or killed in the 5, 10, or 15 years to follow, but also the final solution, Hitler's idea of the elimination of Jews, all of these policies hung together in theory and in practice, with the idea of an invasion of the Soviet Union, the major goal of which would be the conquest of Ukraine.

Consequences of the German occupation of Ukraine

The result was catastrophic for Ukraine: 3.5 million inhabitants of Soviet Ukraine, civilians, were victims of German killing policies between 1941 and 1945. In addition to that 3.5 million Ukrainians died as soldiers in the Red Army, or died indirectly as a consequence of the war.

Of course, the numbers are greater when one includes the entire Soviet Union. But it's worth being specific here about the difference between Ukraine and the rest of the Soviet Union, for two reasons. Ukraine was the center of Hitler's ideological colonialism. But beyond that all of Soviet Ukraine was occupied for most of the war, while German armies never occupied any more than 5% of Soviet Russia, and that for a relatively brief period of time.

Without any doubt the Russian and Ukrainian peoples suffered in WWII in a way that is unthinkable to West Europeans. But nevertheless, when we think about the Soviet Union, the place of Soviet Ukraine is very special, even by comparison to Soviet Russia. In absolute numbers, according to calculations of Russian historians, more inhabitants of Soviet Ukraine died in WWII than inhabitants of Soviet Russia. Which means, in relative terms, Ukraine was far more at risk than Soviet Russia during the war.

In other words, it is very important to think of the German *Vernichtungskrieg* against the Soviet Union. But at the center of this *Vernichtungskrieg* was not only Soviet Russia, but mainly Ukraine.

So if we want to talk about German responsibility for Russia, we must begin with Ukraine. The greatest destructive practice of the German war was precisely in Ukraine. If one is going to be serious for German historical responsibility for the East, the word "Ukraine" must be in the first sentence.

German historical responsibility starts with Ukraine

The Holocaust is organically connected to the *Vernichtungskrieg* of 1941, and to the attempt to conquer Ukraine. Had Hitler not had the colonial idea to fight a war in Eastern Europe to control Ukraine, there could not have been a Holocaust. Because it is that plan that brings German power into Eastern Europe where the Jews lived.

The actual war in Ukraine brings the *Wehrmacht*, brings the SS and the German police to the places where they could be killed. It became clear to Germans in 1941 that something like a Holocaust could be perpetrated because of massacres in places like Kamianets-Podilsky, or, more notoriously, Babyn Yar on the edge of Kyiv. It was there that for the first time in the history of humanity, tens of thousands of people were killed by bullets in a continuous large-scale massacre. It was events like this on the territory of Ukraine that made it clear that something like a Holocaust could happen.

What does this mean? It means that every German who takes seriously the idea of responsibility for the Holocaust must also take seriously the history of the German occupation of Ukraine.

German Judgements about Ukraine are not innocent

As a historian, I know the history of Ukraine is unfamiliar, and it can seem complicated. But this is not the only problem. Part of the problem has to do with habits of mind related to colonization, wars of aggression, to the attempt to enslave another people. The attempt to enslave another people cannot be innocent even for the generations to come. The attempt to enslave another people will leave its mark, if not directly confronted.

There are lots of reasons, but one of them is the mental temptations left over by colonization, the tendency to overlook a people, which was not regarded as a people. All of the language about Ukraine as a *failed state,* or Ukrainians *not as a real nation*, or Ukrainians *divided by culture* – in the German language, that is not innocent. That is an inheritance of an attempt to colonize a people not regarded as a people.

Judgements about Ukraine where Ukraine is held to other standards, but the application of terms like there *not being a Ukrainian nation*, or there *not being a Ukrainian state*, if those things are said in German, those words are not innocent.

I can say this from recent experience as an American: if you get the history of colonization and slavery wrong, it can come back. And your history with Ukraine is precisely the history of colonization and slavery.

Not to help Ukraine, but to help Germany

When I was in Ukraine in September 2016, talking about Babyn Yar, when I was standing in front of millions of Ukrainian television viewers trying to talk about these things in Ukrainian, the point that I tried to make was: you don't remember Babyn Yar for the Jews. You remember Babyn Yar for yourselves. You remember the Holocaust in Ukraine because of its part in building up a responsible civil society and, hopefully in the future, of a functioning democracy in Ukraine. That holds for them, but it also holds for me, and all of us.

The point of remembering German responsibility for the 6.5 million deaths caused by the German war against the Soviet Union in Ukraine is not to help Ukraine. Ukrainians are aware of these crimes. Ukrainians live, the children and grandchildren and great-grandchildren of that generation, they live with the legacy of these crimes already.

It is much more to help Germany. Germany as a democracy, particularly in this historical moment, as we face a declining and decreasingly democratic USA. Precisely at this moment, Germany cannot afford to get major issues of its history wrong. Precisely at this moment, the German sense of responsibility has to be completed.

Getting the history of Ukraine wrong in 2013 and 2014 had European consequences. Getting the history of Ukraine wrong now, when Germany is the leading democracy in the West, will have international consequences.

Chapter 1

Stalinist Repressions

Red Famine

Anne Applebaum

Preface[1]

The warning signs were ample. By the early spring of 1932, the peasants of Ukraine were beginning to starve. Secret police reports and letters from the grain-growing districts all across the Soviet Union – the North Caucases, the Volga region, western Siberia – spoke of children swollen with hunger; of families eating grass and acorns; of peasants fleeing their homes in search of food. In March a medical commission found corpses lying on the street in a village near Odesa. No one was strong enough to bury them. In another village local authorities were trying to conceal the mortality from outsiders. They denied what was happening, even as it was unfolding before their visitors' eyes.

Some wrote directly to the Kremlin, asking for an explanation:

> Honourable Comrade Stalin, is there a Soviet government law stating that villagers should go hungry? Because we, collective farm workers, have not had a slice of bread in our farm since January 1 [...] How can we build a socialist peoples' economy when we are condemned to starving to death, as the harvest is still four months away? What did we die for on the battle-fronts? To go hungry, to see our children die in pangs of hunger?

Others found it impossible to believe the Soviet state could be responsible:

> Every day, ten to twenty families die from famine in the villages, children run off and railway stations are overflowing with fleeing villagers. There are no horses or livestock left in the countryside [...] The bourgeoisie has created a genuine famine here, part of the capitalist plan to set the entire peasant class against the Soviet government.

---

1   Russian and Belarusian place names are transliterated according to the rules of those languages. A few well-known names and place names, including Moscow and Odesa, have been left in their better-known forms, also to make them recognizable to English-language readers.

But the bourgeoisie had not created the famine. The Soviet Union's disastrous decision to force peasants to give up their land and join collective farms; the eviction of "kulaks," the wealthier peasants, from their homes; the chaos that followed; these policies, all ultimately the responsibility of Joseph Stalin, the General Secretary of the Soviet Communist Party, had led the countryside to the brink of starvation. Throughout the spring and summer of 1932, many of Stalin's colleagues sent him urgent messages from all around the USSR, describing the crisis. Communist Party leaders in Ukraine were especially desperate, and several wrote him long letters, begging him for help.

Many of them believed, in the late summer of 1932, that a greater tragedy could still be avoided. The regime could have asked for international assistance, as it had during a previous famine in 1921. It could have halted grain exports, or stopped the punishing grain requisitions altogether. It could have offered aid to peasants in starving regions — and to a degree it did, but not nearly enough.

Instead, in the autumn of 1932, the Soviet Politburo, the elite leadership of the Soviet Communist Party, took a series of decisions that widened and deepened the famine in the Ukrainian countryside and at the same time prevented peasants from leaving the republic in search of food. At the height of the crisis, organized teams of policemen and party activists, motivated by hunger, fear and a decade of hateful and conspiratorial rhetoric, entered peasant households and took everything edible: potatoes, beets, squash, beans, peas, anything in the oven and anything in the cupboard, farm animals and pets.

The result was a catastrophe: At least 5 million people perished of hunger between 1931 and 1934 all across the Soviet Union. Among them were more than 3.9 million Ukrainians. In acknowledgement of its scale, the famine of 1932–3 was described in émigré publications at the time and later as the *Holodomor*, a term derived from the Ukrainian words for hunger — *holod* — and extermination — *mor*.[4]

But famine was only half the story. While peasants were dying in the countryside, the Soviet secret police simultaneously launched an attack on the Ukrainian intellectual and political elites. As the famine spread, a campaign of slander and repression was launched against Ukrainian intellectuals, professors, museum curators, writers, artists, priests, theologians, public officials and bureaucrats. Anyone connected to the short-lived Ukrainian People's Republic, which had existed for a few months from June 1917, anyone who had promoted the Ukrainian language or Ukrainian history, anyone with an independent literary or artistic career, was liable to be publicly vilified, jailed, sent to a labour camp or executed. Unable to watch what was happening, Mykola Skrypnyk, one of the best-known leaders of the Ukrainian Communist Party, committed suicide in 1933. He was not alone.

Taken together, these two policies—the Holodomor in the winter and spring of 1933 and the repression of the Ukrainian intellectual and political class in the months that followed—brought about the Sovietization of Ukraine, the destruction of the Ukrainian national idea, and the neutering of any Ukrainian challenge to Soviet unity. Raphael Lemkin, the Polish-Jewish lawyer who invented the word "genocide," spoke of Ukraine in this era as the "classic example" of his concept: "It is a case of genocide, of destruction, not of individuals only, but of a culture and a nation." Since Lemkin first coined the term, "genocide" has come to be used in a narrower, more legalistic way. It has also become a controversial touchstone, a concept used by both Russians and Ukrainians, as well as by different groups within Ukraine, to make political arguments. For that reason, a separate discussion of the Holodomor as a "genocide" — as well as Lemkin's Ukrainian connections and influences—forms part of the epilogue to this book.

The central subject is more concrete: what actually happened in Ukraine between the years 1917 and 1934? In particular, what happened in the autumn, winter and spring of 1932–3? What chain of events, and what mentality, led to the famine? Who was responsible? How does this terrible episode fit into the broader history of Ukraine and of the Ukrainian national movement?

Just as importantly: what happened afterwards? The Sovietization of Ukraine did not begin with the famine and did not end with it. Arrests of Ukrainian intellectuals and leaders continued through the 1930s. For more than half a century after that, successive Soviet leaders continued to push back harshly against Ukrainian nationalism in whatever form it took, whether as post-war insurgency or as dissent in the 1980s. During those years Sovietization often took the form of Russification: the Ukrainian language was demoted, Ukrainian history was not taught.

Above all, the history of the famine of 1932–3 was not taught. Instead, between 1933 and 1991 the USSR simply refused to acknowledge that any famine had ever taken place. The Soviet state destroyed local archives, made sure that death records did not allude to starvation, even altered publicly available census data in order to conceal what had happened. As long as the USSR existed, it was not possible to write a fully documented history of the famine and the accompanying repression.

But in 1991 Stalin's worst fear came to pass. Ukraine did declare independence. The Soviet Union did come to an end, partly as the result of Ukraine's decision to leave it. A sovereign Ukraine came into being for the first time in history, along with a new generation of Ukrainian historians, archivists, journalists and publishers. Thanks to their efforts, the complete story of the famine of 1932–3 can now be told.

This book begins in 1917, with the Ukrainian revolution and the Ukrainian national movement that was destroyed in 1932–3. It ends in the present, with a discussion of the ongoing politics of memory in Ukraine. It focuses on the famine in Ukraine, which, although part of a wider Soviet famine, had unique causes and attributes. The historian Andrea Graziosi has noted that nobody confuses the general history of "Nazi atrocities" with the very specific story of Hitler's persecution of Jews or gypsies. By the same logic, this book discusses the Soviet-wide famines between 1930 and 1934 — which also led to high death rates, especially in Kazakhstan and particular provinces of Russia — but focuses more directly on the specific tragedy of Ukraine.

The book also reflects a quarter-century's worth of scholarship on Ukraine. In the early 1980s, Robert Conquest compiled everything then publicly available about the famine, and the book he published in 1986, *The Harvest of Sorrow*, still stands as a landmark in writing about the Soviet Union. But in the three decades since the end of the USSR and the emergence of a sovereign Ukraine, several broad national campaigns to collect oral history and memoirs have yielded thousands of new testimonies from all over the country. During that same time period, archives in Kyiv—unlike those in Moscow—have become accessible and easy to use; the percentage of unclassified material in Ukraine is one of the highest in Europe. Ukrainian government funding has encouraged scholars to publish collections of documents, which have made research even more straightforward. Established scholars on the famine and on the Stalinist period in Ukraine—among them Olga Bertelsen, Hennadii Boriak, Vasyl Danylenko, Lyudmyla Hrynevych, Roman Krutsyk, Stanislav Kulchytsky,

Yuri Mytsyk, Vasyl Marochko, Heorhii Papakin, Ruslan Pyrih, Yuri Shapoval, Volodymyr Serhiichuk, Valerii Vasylyev, Oleksandra Veselova and Hennadii Yefimenko—have produced multiple books and monographs, including collections of reprinted documents as well as oral history. Oleh Wolowyna and a team of demographers—Oleksander Hladun, Natalia Levchuk, Omelian Rudnytsky—have at last begun to do the difficult work of establishing the numbers of victims. The Harvard Ukrainian Research Institute has worked with many of these scholars to publish and publicize their work.

The Holodomor Research and Education Consortium in Toronto, led by Marta Baziuk, and its partner organization in Ukraine, led by Lyudmyla Hrynevych, continue to fund new scholarship. Younger scholars are opening new lines of inquiry too. Daria Mattingly's research on the motives and background of the people who confiscated food from starving peasants and Tetiana Boriak's work on oral history both stand out; they also contributed important research to this book. Western scholars have made new contributions too. Lynne Viola's archival work on collectivization and the subsequent peasant rebellion have altered the perceptions of the 1930s. Terry Martin was the first to reveal the chronology of the decisions Stalin took in the autumn of 1932—and Timothy Snyder and Andrea Graziosi were among the first to recognize their significance. Serhii Plokhy and his team at Harvard have launched an unusual effort to map the famine, the better to understand how it happened. I am grateful to all of these for the scholarship and in some cases the friendship that contributed so much to this project.

Perhaps if this book had been written in a different era, this very brief introduction to a complex subject could end here. But because the famine destroyed the Ukrainian national movement, because that movement was revived in 1991, and because the leaders of modern Russia still challenge the legitimacy of the Ukrainian state, I should note here that I first discussed the need for a new history of the famine with colleagues at the Harvard Ukrainian Research Institute in 2010. Viktor Yanukovych had just been elected president of Ukraine, with Russian backing and support. Ukraine then attracted little political attention from the rest of Europe, and almost no press coverage at all. At that moment, there was no reason to think that a fresh examination of 1932–3 would be interpreted as a political statement of any kind.

The Maidan revolution of 2014, Yanukovych's decision to shoot at protesters and then flee the country, the Russian invasion and annexation of Crimea, the Russian invasion of eastern Ukraine and the accompanying Russian propaganda campaign—all unexpectedly put Ukraine at the centre of international politics while I was working on this book. My research on Ukraine was actually delayed by events in that country, both because I wrote about them and because my Ukrainian colleagues were so transfixed by what was happening. But while the events of that year put Ukraine at the heart of world politics, this book was not written in reaction to them. Nor is it an argument for or against any Ukrainian politician or party, or a reaction to what is happening in Ukraine today. It is instead an attempt to tell the story of the famine using new archives, new testimony and new research, to draw together the work of the extraordinary scholars listed above.

This is not to say that the Ukrainian revolution, the early years of Soviet Ukraine, the mass repression of the Ukrainian elite as well as the Holodomor do not have a relationship to current events. On the contrary: they are the crucial backstory that underlies and explains them. The famine and its legacy play an enormous role in contemporary Russian and Ukrainian arguments about their identity, their relationship and their shared Soviet experience. But before describing those arguments or weighing their merits, it is important to understand, first, what actually happened.

Holodomor
Understanding the History and Significance of the Great Ukrainian Famine[1]

Serhii Plokhy

"In almost every village, the bread supply had run out two months earlier, the potatoes were almost exhausted, and there was not enough coarse beet, which was formerly used as cattle fodder, but has now become a staple food of the population, to last until the next harvest," wrote Gareth Jones, a Walsh journalist and the main character in Agnieszka Holland's movie "Mr. Jones" to the editor of the *Manchester Guardian* in March 1933. He described what he had seen a few weeks earlier in rural Ukraine. He continued: "One phrase was repeated until it had a sad monotony in my mind, and that was: "Vse opukhli" ("all are swollen from hunger"), and one word was drummed into my memory by every talk. That word was "golod", meaning "hunger" or "famine". Nor shall I forget the swollen stomachs of the children in the cottages in which I slept."

Walter Duranty, a Pulitzer Prize winning *New York Times* reporter and the antagonist of Mr. Jones in Holland's movie, attacked him in one of his articles, claiming that Jones who traveled in early 1933 to Ukraine presented in his accounts "a rather inadequate cross section of a big country." Duranty admitted "food shortages" but not famine. Indeed, while the food shortages were an all-Union phenomenon, the famine was not. It hit mostly, but not exclusively, the grain producing areas of the Soviet Union, including the lower Volga region with its Russian majority and German minority, which suffered the most, and the Kuban region of the North Caucasus, which was largely settled by Ukrainians. Ukraine however was hit the hardest, the death toll there reaching four million peo-

---

1   This article draws on the author's earlier works on the subject.

ple, more than half of those who starved to death in the Soviet Union during that period.

In Ukraine the famine of 1932-1933 is known today as the Holodomor, or the 'death by hunger." The immediate cause of the famine was Stalin's drive to gain control over the Soviet Union's agricultural sector in order to finance his ambitious industrialization and militarization plans. This meant forcing millions of peasants onto collective farms. The regime singled Ukraine, the proverbial "breadbasket of Europe" out for especially harsh treatment, as it was crucial to the fulfillment of Moscow's economic plans. By mid-1932, 70 percent of Ukraine's households were collectivized, as opposed to an average of 60 percent across the Soviet Union. The republic that produced 27 percent of Soviet grain became responsible for 38 percent of all grain deliveries to the state.

As resistance to collectivization grew in the spring of 1930, Ukraine became a focal point of peasant uprisings. Faced with this new form of peasant resistance, Stalin and his aides refused to admit defeat and accused the peasants of sabotage and attempting to starve the cities and undermine industrialization. The authorities declared that the peasants were hiding grain and used the police to exile the troublemakers and well to do peasants ("kulaks" or "kurkuls") and forced the rest into the collective farms. The new policy brought famine and mass starvation to Ukraine in the winter and spring of 1932. By the fall of 1932 the entire republic was bracing itself for the new and much larger wave of hunger.

Stalin used the crisis to crush what he considered to be Ukrainian nationalism, manifested in Ukrainian resistance to collectivization, both within and outside of Ukraine. He believed the cultural accommodation of Ukrainians during the early years of the Soviet Union had strengthened rather than weakened their resistance to the regime. It was an error he sought to correct. On December 14, 1932, he signed a decree titled "On the Procurement of Grain in Ukraine, the North Caucasus, and the Western Region." The decree aimed to mobilize party cadres to continue extracting grain from the countryside so that it among other things could be sold abroad to pay for Soviet industrialization. The Soviet leaders demanded that their underlings in Ukraine and the North Caucasus — two out of three main grain-producing areas of the USSR – fulfill the grain-procurement plans for 1932 by January–February 1933.

The decree of December 14 also dealt with the politics of culture. All "saboteurs" listed by name were Soviet cadres from Ukraine, and the population of the Poltavskaia village in the Kuban region condemned for exile to the Soviet north happened to be overwhelmingly Ukrainian as well. The decree ordered local officials in Kuban to change the language of their official correspondence and of public education immediately from Ukrainian to Russian and to stop publishing Ukrainian-language newspapers and journals. In Ukraine, the decree demanded that the republic's leaders establish strict control over the "Ukrainization" policy instituted in the 1920s to promote the development of Ukrainian culture, as well as to purge nationalists and agents of foreign powers. Hundreds of Ukrainian party and cultural cadres were fired, arrested and exiled, while some of the key promoters of the Ukrainianization policies like the People's Commissar of Education Mykola Skrypnyk, and Ukraine's leading communist writer Mykola Khvyliovy committed suicides.

Led by Moscow plenipotentiaries and terrorized by Stalin's secret police, local authorities took all they could from the starving and, in many cases, dying peasantry. The authorities punished those villages that failed to fulfill their quotas by cutting off supplies of basic goods, including matches and kerosene, and confiscating not only grain but also livestock and anything else that could be used as food. The first cases of mass death from starvation were recorded that same January. Especially hard hit were regions of central Ukraine that had not recovered from the famine of 1932. Peasants there died at a higher rate than anywhere else, most of them succumbing to death between March and June 1933, when food supplies were exhausted and early crops turned out to be too difficult for starving stomachs to digest. Government assistance arrived too late and was insufficient to stop the death spiral.

Other grain-producing areas of the USSR also experienced famine, but in contrast to Russia, the famine in Ukraine was not restricted to grain-producing regions. The impact of the Holodomor extended to parts of the country that were never considered part of the fabled Ukrainian breadbasket. This included the Kharkiv and Kyiv regions in Ukraine's forest-steppe zone. More than half of the estimated four million Ukrainians who lost their lives in the famine perished in regions that did not belong to the country's grain-producing agricultural heartlands. The only reason these areas suffered so badly was because they were part of Ukraine, which in administrative, cultural and political terms was treated by Moscow as one unit.

The famine dramatically changed Ukrainian society and culture, leaving deep scars in the national memory. It also produced a vast literature on the subject and generated numerous debates in Ukraine and beyond. As the Soviet regime refused to admit the very existence of the famine, its recognition was hotly contested in the last decades of the Cold War. Since the collapse of the Soviet Union, the discussion has centered on whether the Holodomor qualifies as an act of genocide against the Ukrainian nation. This was the definition given to the famine and the attack on the Ukrainian culture that accompanied it by no less an authority than Raphael Lemkin, the lawyer who coined the term "genocide". In November 2006, the Ukrainian parliament defined it as such. A number of parliaments and governments around the world passed similar resolutions, while the Russian government launched an international campaign to undermine the Ukrainian claim.

Political controversy and scholarly debate on the nature of the Ukrainian famine continue to this day, turning largely on the definition of the term "genocide." But a broad consensus is also emerging on some of the crucial facts and interpretations of the 1932–1933 famine. Most scholars agree that it was indeed a man-made phenomenon caused by official policy; while it also affected the North Caucasus, the lower Volga region, and Kazakhstan, only in Ukraine did it result from policies with clear ethnonational coloration and targeted not only the peasantry but also the new political class and the cultural elite. The regime was not only going after Ukrainian grain; it was also targeting Ukrainian culture and, ultimately, Ukrainian identity itself.

Executed Renaissance
What the Ukrainian Intelligentsia's Fate in the USSR Can Tell Us about Our World Today

Volodymyr Yermolenko

***

On 13 May, 1933, at 11 am, Mykola Khvyliovyi, one of the key leaders of Ukrainian Soviet writers, invited fellow writers Mykola Kulish and Oles' Dosvitnyi to his apartment. Together with his wife, Yulia Umantseva, he wanted to discuss the arrest of Khvyliovyi's friend, writer Mykhaylo Yalovyi. The detention of Yalovyi was not alone: it followed arrests of other Ukrainian writers and was a sign of decisiveness of Soviet repressive authorities to annihilate Ukrainian intelligentsia in the Soviet Union—considered to be too free-thinking to be really "Soviet".

During this meeting Khvyliovyi, quite probably, also discussed with his guests what he saw during his trips to villages in the nearby Poltava region: the Famine (Holodomor) organized by Stalin regime against Ukrainian peasants, leaving about 4 million people dead in 1932-1933.

At one moment Khvyliovyi left his guests and went to another room. He stayed there for quite a while. He wrote something on two pieces of paper.

Then he shot himself.

"Yalovyi arrest is an execution of the whole generation," — these were his final words.

Khvyliovyi was right. After his suicide, most of his fellow writers, including Kulish and Dosvitnyi present in his apartment in the morning of May 13th, were arrested. Many of them were executed in 1937 in Gulag camps.

Khvyliovyi shot himself in the house "Slovo" ("Word"), built specifically for the Ukrainian Soviet writers in Kharkiv,. The building, constructed in 1930, in a form of a letter C (the first letter in the word «Слово», "Word"), was a "cooperative" home to several dozens Ukrainian Soviet writers. You can still find it Kharkiv, on the address 9, vul. Kultury, but there is little which reminds about its dramatic past—except for a memorial board on one of its walls. Dwellers of about 40 apartments out of 66 of the Slovo house were victims of Stalinist repressions.

The "generation" Khvyliovyi referred to, was later called "Executed Renaissance"—or "Executed Regeneration"—a term invented in 1950s by Polish intellectual Jerzy Giedroyc, the founder of Polish Paris-based émigré journal *Kultura*. The term was used by Ukrainian literary historian Yuriy Lavrinenko as a title of his anthology book published by Paris-based Giedroyc-led *Instytut Literacki* in 1959.

The term was very pertinent metaphor implying that the Ukrainian cultural renaissance in 1920s was brutally destroyed, majority of its representatives were sent to camps and killed, and Ukrainian future was amputated.

But it had a specific echo with Khvyliovyi himself, for whom the word "renaissance" had a deep meaning, rooted in the history of the European culture.

***

Eight years before his suicide, in 1925, Khvyliovyi published a book of essays "Quo Vadis?" («Камо Грядеши?»). In one of these essays he was saying that the young proletarian culture in Soviet Ukraine meant something big for Europe as a whole. Western Europe had its Renaissance in the 15th-16th century; now similar process is taking place in Eastern Europe, Khvyliovyi said. This is the process he was calling an "Asian Renaissance". What he meant was that values developed by the European culture are now expanding to the East. They will break through Europe's Eastern borders and inject the European cultural heritage to "Asia"; and Ukraine will be among the "doors" through which cultural Europe will move to the East.

By the concept of "Asian Renaissance" Khvyliovyi was making a great effort of rethinking both Ukrainian and European cultural traditions. He tried to make Ukrainian culture much less pro-vincial than Soviet dogma was wishing it to be. He tried to anchor Ukrainian leftist literature of the 1920s in the global phenomena of the European intellectual and cultural history, primarily in the con-cept of "Renaissance" of 15th-16th century Europe.

At the same time, he was trying to think the dynamic capacity of the European culture itself. He did think that the Soviet culture of the 1920s was suggesting something fresh and new for the Euro-pean context as a whole. The proletarian revolution was giving a new chance to Europe too, he believed, and Ukraine was set to play a special role *precisely because* its culture has been earlier repeatedly eradicated. Ukraine has lost its aristocracy in various epochs of its modern history, assimilated by Polish or Russian states; it barely had its own bourgeoisie—and Khvyliovyi was trying to transform these huge problems into benefits. It is precisely because Ukraine—contrary even to Russia—doesn't have its aristocratic past and bourgeois present, that it will be able to give floor to a genuinely "bottom-up" culture, proletarian culture able to create something radically new, he thought.

This thinking about Soviet revolution in the global context, as a continuation of a great European tradition rather than the oppo-sition to it, was something that could have given much more hu-manity to the Soviet political and cultural project—although its cruel sides were showing themselves well before Stalinism, and Ukrainians knew this very well.

However, after Stalin took over power in the Soviet Union, af-ter he declared his "great turn" in 1929, no dreams about human-istic proletarian culture could have been taken seriously. The con-flict of Khvyliovyi generation and Stalinism was inevitable: their world views and values were completely different. Khvyliovyi was dreaming about European values moving to the East; Stalin was dreaming about totalitarian Soviet values moving to the West.

A shot on May 13th 1933 in the house "Slovo" in Kharkiv was not only a personal tragedy of one Ukrainian Soviet writer. It was something bigger than even the "execution of the whole genera-tion" as Khvyliovyi described it. It had much more global meaning: it was one of the points where Soviet Union was showing that it is not a continuation of humanistic Europe, but its radical opponent, its dark demonic shadow, which at one day will be able to absorb Europe itself — or at least part of it. In 1933 Europe was no longer moving to the East. Very soon, already in 1939, and moreover after 1945, Europe saw a totalitarian East moving to the West.

***

In his debate of the 1920s Khvyliovyi had an unusual ally: Mykola Zerov. Zerov was not a "proletarian" writer (he was born in a family of a school teacher) and not a political essayist: he was a classical philologist and a university professor. He was a popular lecturer, a historian of the Ukrainian literature, a poet and a translator of ancient Roman and modern European literature. He was also a key representative of the "neo-classicist school" of the Ukrainian poetry.

In 1926 Zerov wrote an essay supporting Khvyliovyi's argument, "Eurasian Renaissance and the Pines of Poshekhonye", launching a concept of "Eurasian renaissance" — more accurate culturally and historically than Khvyliovyi's "Asian Renaissance". But its argument was very close to that of Khvyliovyi: "let's not avoid the old Europe, neither the bourgeois Europe, nor even the feudal one", Zerov said, hinting that the young "ex nihilo" proletarian culture should not neglect the big European heritage — even if it thought to be ideologically alien to itself.

Zerov was arrested in April, 1935. He was executed in November 1937, in Sandarmokh in a Gulag camp in Karelia, 1500 km to the north from his Kyiv home, with thousands of other prisoners, including several dozens representatives of Ukrainian intelligentsia. Even in the camps, he was translating Virgil's *Aeneid* from Latin into Ukrainian.

***

Most of the writers arrested in the 1930s, were convicted — imagine this! — for terrorism. Translating Virgil from Latin, putting plays on stage or reforming the Ukrainian language was thought to be "terrorism" by then Soviet repression machine.

Khvyliovyi friends playwright Mykola Kulish (who was present in Khvyliovyi apartment during the suicide) and theatre director Les' Kurbas faced an especially cynical accusation. OGPU accused Kurbas, the prominent founder and director of a modern Ukrainian theatre *Berezil'*, in planning a terrorist act against the leaders of the Communist party during the premiere of the new theatrical season, on a play by Mykola Kulish. Through torture and intimidation they made people invent fantastic stories about plots, turning writers and playwrights into radical extremists knowing how to operate with guns and explosive materials. Kulish and Kurbas were executed in Sandarmokh on the same day as Mykola Zerov, in November 1937.

***

The tragedy of the 1930s was neither the beginning nor the end of the story.

It was preceded by other repressions. Before 1933, was the year of 1930, the fabricated trial against the "SVU" — the Union for Ukraine's Liberation; the trial was attacking those writers and artists who were linked to the Ukrainian independence of 1917-1921. Some of the later representatives of proletarian "executed Renaissance" — like Oleksa Slisarenko — were actually participating in the SVU process on the side of accusers. Like it often happened in Stalin's times, the accusers were soon be turned into victims (Slisarenko was also killed in November 1937 in Sandarmokh).

But it was not the end either. Holodomor took lives of about 4 million Ukrainian peasants. In 1932-1937, as we have seen, majority of Ukrainian free-thinking leftist intelligentsia were arrested and executed. 1930s also started a long process of "linguocide", through which Ukrainian language, although formally "allowed" (contrary to the late 19th century Russian empire) was artificially approximated to the Russian language. For example, through dictionaries, in which genuine Ukrainian words were suppressed or marked as obsolete or dialectical, and where the first "Ukrainian" word to be suggested as a translation of the Russian word was usually an artificial copy of the latter.

But repressions also continued throughout the 20th century, especially after short-lived Khrushchiov's "ottepel". Some of Ukrainian artists were killed (like painter Alla Horska) or severely beaten which led to their death (like poet Vasyl Symonenko). Others were sent to camps — like Stus, Chornovil, Rudenko, Sverstiuk, Marynovych, Lisovyi, Svitlychnyi, and dozens of others. Others were declared "psychically ill" like Leonid Plushch or trialed for homosexualism, like world-famous cinema director Paradzhanov.

The battle is therefore not over. And we don't know whether it will be over any time soon.

***

Studying the stories of Ukrainian literary renaissance of the 1920s, and its execution in the 1930s, is much more than an exercise in literary history. It can give important hints to understand the situation today.

First, it shows that Ukrainian national movement has been ideologically diverse. Russian propaganda tries to show this movement as variations of the "far-right" or "fascist" idea. The "fascism" narrative was developed back then, already in the 1930s, and before writers like Zerov, Kulish, Kurbas and dozens of others were executed in northern Russian camps, OGPU was spreading the internal reports that it found a "fascist" group among Ukrainian prisoners. Today, Russian propaganda keeps naming post-Maidan Ukraine as a "fascist" state — precisely because it has much more in common with the writers who died in the 1930s, than with their killers.

The truth is, however, that writers executed in 1937 were anything but fascists. They were *leftist* writers, convinced that the communist idea is true; quite often, they trusted it too much, at least in the 1920s. Moreover, people whom they found in camps, imprisoned before them — active figures in the Ukrainian short-lived independence of 1917-1921 — were also most often *leftists*, although not dogmatic communists as someone wanted them to be.

Decades later, Ukrainian Soviet dissidents of the 1970s-1980s like Stus or Rudenko were anything but fascists too. They were liberals — or patriotic liberals, one could say — convinced that the Soviet Union is criminal because it violates human rights on an enormous scale. They were arguing that USSR, after it signed Helsinki Final Act, need to observe its principles.

So, Ukrainian national movement was leftist in 1910s-1920s, when to be "progressive" in the whole Europe meant to be socialist. It was more inclined to the "rightwing" and even "far-right" spectrum in the 1930s when the whole Europe was thinking in terms of extreme right vs extreme left confrontation. And it became liberal — or human-rights oriented — in 1970s, when human rights topic in the whole Europe began pushing out the communist idea.

The second lesson from the fate of Ukrainian writers of 1920s — is that the approaches and the rhetoric of Russian repressive services (OGPU, NKVD, KGB or FSB) do not change much since then. In 1930s, OGPU arrested Ukrainian theatre director Les' Kurbas and accused him of terrorism; in 2010s, FSB arrested Ukrainian cinema director Oleh Sentsov and accused him of terrorism. Did anything change that much?

And the third lesson is about geopolitics. Khvyliovyi, who shot himself in his Kharkiv apartment in 1933, was dreaming about the "enlargement" of European values — what he called "psychological Europe" (which we now would probably call "axiological Europe") — to the East. His major point was that Europe's cultural capacity, expressed in its full strength in the Renaissance of the 15th-16th centuries, can work again in Eastern Europe, in a new country and in a new culture. He believed that Europe's borders are not political, and that European values are enlarging to other parts of the world faster than European political institutions.

In a way, this sentiment was driving Ukraine's Euromaidan in 2013-2014, and Ukrainians' fight against Russian aggression since then. It has also been driving Belarusian protests since August 2020 (+ editors' note). Their key driver is a value of dignity, key for the European Union (look at article 2 of its treaty) — but now also to Eastern European societies which the EU is bordering.

The story of the 1920s-1930s can teach us that "dreams of Europe" — dreams of the European values enlarging to the Eastern Europe — can be born in this part of the world, can pose a threat to authoritarian regimes, can be target of cynical attacks from these regimes, can be eradicated, — but then again, can be reborn, decades later.

Ukrainian "Executed Renaissance" of the 1920s, with its clear universalist vector, seeking the foundations of the Ukrainian culture in the universal European culture, is therefore an important anchor to understand development of history today. History is not repeating itself literally, but it often suggests variations around similar questions and similar answers.

Will the "dreams of Europe" of Eastern European countries attain their goal? Or, instead, will they lose — and the expansion of anti-Europe will win against the European project? Will the tragedies of the 1930s repeat today?

We don't know the answer. But the question is vitally crucial. For the whole societies to the East of the EU, it is the question of life and death.

Germans Search for Their Heritage in Declassified Ukrainian Archives

Oksana Grytsenko

Brick houses under tiled roofs, brightly colored old factory buildings, graves with Latin inscriptions. These remnants of a German community can be found in many Ukrainian cities and villages, while there are almost no Germans living there anymore. But these old bricks are precious for many descendants of Ukrainian Germans.

Irina Peter remembers that when she visited Gottliebsdorf, a German settlement near Korosten in Zhytomyr Oblast, where her ancestors come from, she couldn't hold back her tears. "I had to cry as if I cried all the tears that my grandparents were not allowed to cry when they were deported in 1936," she said.

Peter was born in Nursultan, the capital of Kazakhstan, where her grandparents were sent by the regime of Soviet dictator Josef Stalin in an attempt to move Germans who lived near the western border of the Soviet Union when a war with Nazi Germany was expected. Peter's family lived since the 19th century in the territory of modern Zhytomyr Oblast, which used to be part of Volhynian Governorate. They were German Lutherans who came there from Eastern Prussia via Poland and were involved in agriculture.

According to the last population census conducted in 2001, there are 33,300 Germans in Ukraine, just a tiny fraction of what was there several decades ago. The population census of 1939 showed that there were more than 627,000 Germans living in Soviet Ukraine only. But most of them were deported to Central Asia or Russia in the following years without permission to come back.

Peter, who emigrated to Germany in 1992, was trying for years to be as German as possible. But thanks to stories told by her grandmother Olga about beautiful Volhynia she started inquiries about her family's past. In 2018, Peter eventually visited Ukraine and searched for her family history in Zhytomyr in the declassified archives of the KGB, the former Soviet secret police. She found her great-great-grandfather's certificate of naturalization there.

Fully opened for the public since 2015, the archives in Ukraine are said to contain the largest set of freely accessible information on the Soviet secret police in Europe, local historians say. Later, the authorities also granted access to the archives of the Soviet police, prisons and prosecutors and made a large part of the Soviet military archives accessible to the public.

Black Sea Germans

At his home in Odesa, a Black Sea port city, Oleksiy Köhler is researching historic documents about local Germans that he copied from local archives. He is also assisting people who look for data about their German ancestors.

"Sometimes I find one card in the archive, and then — based on it — a person discovers papers about five to seven generations of his ancestors," Köhler said. "Then people find the exact names in church books and can write the history of their families or prove their German roots."

Köhler has been searching archives since the 1990s, when he headed a local German heritage organization (deutsche Gebietsgesellschaft "Wiedergeburt"). The archives helped him to dig out the history of his family members, German colonists who came to the Russian Empire from the territory of Baden-Württemberg state.

"A few years ago I found the ID number (Ausweisnummer) of my great grandfather Carl Köhler. He arrived in Ukraine in 1809 and lived in a colony called Sulz, which existed on the territory of the modern Mykolayiv Oblast," he said.

Russian tsars invited Germans to settle in the sparsely populated Black Sea area, granting them free land, religious freedoms, and tax exemptions. The area between the Dnister and South Buh Rivers, where Odesa and Mykolayiv oblasts are located now, had more than 400 German settlements, Köhler said. But when the Russian Empire was replaced by the Soviet Union, the new authorities usually cracked down on well-established German colonists and started repressions against them. Köhler's grandfather was sent to prison in 1937, the year of the biggest Stalin's repression.

At the end of World War II, most Germans living in southern Ukraine (so-called Volksdeutsche) were sent by retreating Nazi troops to the territory of modern Poland. After the war, the Soviets sent them back to the USSR and deported them predominantly to Siberia or Central Asia.

Köhler's father, who was just seven back then, was deported to Ivanovo Oblast in central Russia to a special camp for interned children, where he was punished for speaking German outside German school classes or correcting his German language teacher. Köhler's father managed to secretly return to Ukraine and settled near Odesa but the family was afraid of disclosing their German origin for years. "My father was afraid to speak German until the 1990s, when the Soviet Union collapsed," Köhler said.

Hidden treasures

It was a common belief that in the 1920-1940s that most of the data about Germans in the Soviet Union was either taken away by Nazis during the war or destroyed by the Soviet secret police. But after the USSR collapsed, historians found hidden treasures in Ukrainian archives.

Köhler recalls that in 1992 he brought his German colleague Alfred Eisfeld to the Odesa Oblast Archive. Eisfeld was astonished to discover that about 200,000 archive documents about the Black Sea Germans were kept there.

Eisfeld, who now heads the Institute of German and Eastern European Studies in Goettingen, said he discovered in Odesa a lot of data about Germans dating back in the 19th and early 20th centuries. He kept traveling to Ukraine and found a lot of other interesting stuff in the archives of Dnipro, Kherson, Mykolayiv, and Simferopol. "We've been discovering the long-forgotten and little researched pages of Ukraine's multinational history," Eisfeld said.

Just like Köhler, Eisfeld was attracted by Germans in Ukraine because of his own family story. Back in the late 18th century, his ancestors came from Germany to Ekaterinoslav Governorate, which is now the territory of Dnipropetrovsk Oblast. Some of them lived in a German colony, Josefstal, which is now located on the outskirts of Dnipro.

Attempts to revive German heritage

In Gottliebsdorf, which used to be totally populated by Germans, Peter found just a few remaining German houses. Now this village has a Ukrainian name, Zorianka. Peter managed to visit one of these single-storey houses and see how its structure is similar to the house where her grandmother lived in Kazakhstan.

Being back in Mannheim, Peter plans to go back to Ukraine and continue researching her family history regardless of its sadness. "I don't like happy ends, so I kind of like the sad stories of my family and try to keep them for the future by writing about them," she said.

In the town of Novhorodske, located in Donetsk Oblast near the frontline of the war between Ukraine and Russian-backed separatists, local activists are trying to revive their German past. This town was created by German Mennonites in the late 19th century and was called New Jork after the town of Jork in northern Germany near Hamburg, where they had come from. Now the name is mostly confused in New York in the United States.

Most Germans were deported from there by the Soviet authorities to Kazakhstan on a single day in October 1941. But their houses remained in a rather good shape. With the help of local businesses and United Nations grants, the local authorities managed to refurbish a former German bookstore this year to establish there a community center called "Ukrainian New Jork," said Tetiana Krasko, the secretary of the town council.

Now they are also developing tourist routes along the main street that used to be called *Gartenstrasse* – a name that reflects the beautiful fruit gardens that were planted there by Germans.

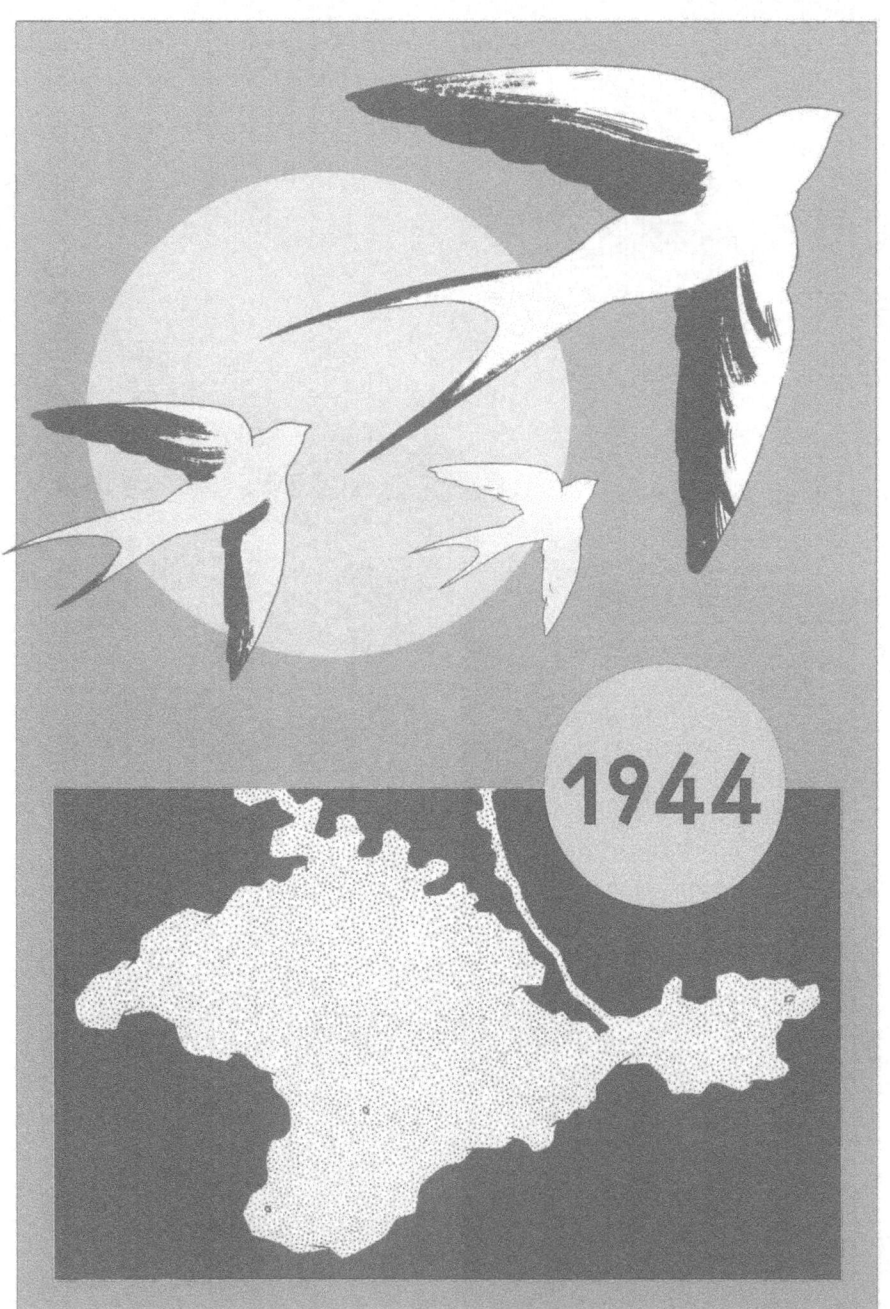

Deportation of Crimean Tatars
A Thorny Path through the Decades

Viktoria Savchuk

In the history of Ukraine, many events are largely unknown abroad. The Soviet era until the proclamation of independence in 1991 was particularly challenging for the country. This period was an era of massive repression, politically motivated persecutions of dissenters and so-called ethnic cleansing of ethnic groups not considered loyal by the Soviet regime.

One of these crimes committed by the Soviet power is still remembered very well by the indigenous Crimean Tatar people on the Ukrainian peninsula of Crimea. It is the 1944 deportation of over 200,000 Crimean Tatars. In 2015, this deportation was recognized by the Ukrainian Parliament as genocide of the Crimean Tatar people. However, to understand the background of this tragedy, it is necessary to return to the events of 1944 briefly.

Background of the deportation

Shortly before Crimea was liberated from the Nazi occupation, which lasted until May 13, 1944, the fate of the Crimean Tatars was discussed in the Moscow Kremlin. The Soviet government planned an action to "cleanse Crimea of anti-Soviet elements" — affecting the entire Crimean Tatar people. The official justification for this can be found in Decree No. 5859-ss of May 11, 1944, on the resettlement of Crimean Tatars in the Uzbek Soviet Republic: They were accused of "treason against the motherland," "desertion of Red Army units," and "mass collaboration with the Nazis."

According to Russian sources, the number of desertions in the fall of 1941 was about 20 000 Crimean Tatars, which is disproportionately high and highly doubtful: A total of about 20,000 Crimean Tatars served in the Red Army — of which no more than 10,000 soldiers took part in hostilities. Historians estimate the number of Crimean Tatar deserters at around 4,000.

Regarding collaboration, however, it must be said that 15,000 to 16,000 Crimean Tatars collaborated with the German occupiers then. It seems important to mention that almost all of them perished or were sentenced to imprisonment. Moreover, collaboration was not a rarity at that time: In the occupied territories, there was usually a certain percentage of the local population — representatives of various (often small) peoples who felt compelled to collaborate with the occupiers under the threat of death or for the safety of their own families. Criminal responsibility, however, should be viewed on an individual basis. The whole people should not be held collectively responsible for crimes certain individuals commit.

Nevertheless, the Crimean Tatar population was deported on May 18, 1944, shortly after adopting the relevant decree, for "urgent resettlement" from their homeland Crimea to remote areas of central Asia, Siberia, and the Urals. All people of Crimean Tatar origin living in Crimea were expelled: women, children and older people. Surprisingly, even the family members of Crimean Tatars, who were highly decorated by the Red Army for their military service, were not exempt. There was no possibility for Crimean Tatar soldiers and officers who had served in other Soviet regions at that time to return to Crimea.

The active phase of the targeted deportation was extraordinarily short: in a single day, the decree was enforced violently by the USSR Ministry of Internal Affairs (or the NKVD) troops. Armed soldiers usually stormed the houses of Crimean Tatars at night or in the early morning, searched them, forced eviction and confiscated remaining property. According to survivors' recollections, many people feared being shot at the time.

> At night the soldiers woke us up with guns and ordered us to leave the house. My father thought we would be shot. Under guard, we were taken to a freight train.
> *Witness Munire, 96 years old, from Bakhchisaray, Crimea, Ukraine.*

The deportees were transported in an inhumane way in overcrowded freight cars. They suffered from hunger, thirst and unsanitary conditions. About 46 percent of the Crimean Tatar population died during the expulsion and in the first years afterward.

> We were thrown into boxcars, everywhere was very dirty. Two people died next to us. We saw the bodies from other wagons being left on the road.
> On June 6, 1944, we were taken to the Hakulabad station in Namangan oblast [area in the then Uzbek Soviet Socialist Republic – author's note]. There was no one else around, as if the village was extinct.
> Contemporary witness Khalide, 92 years old, from Yalta, Crimea, Ukraine.

It should be mentioned here that the expulsion policy of that time affected not only the Crimean Tatar people. For the same reasons, in 1944, the Soviet government also expelled from Crimea about 16,000 people of Greek nationality, 12,500 people of Bulgarian nationality and almost 10,000 people of Armenian nationality.

Based on these facts, it can be assumed that the real purpose of the 1944 mass deportations was the maximum "cleansing" of Crimea. The peninsula was to become "free" of undesirable and anti-Soviet elements – of Crimean Tatar and other nationalities – who could initiate "anti-Soviet movements" or, in case of a Soviet attack on Turkey, support the latter. Moreover, mass deportation seemed to be an "effective" measure to provide other regions of the Union with additional cheap labor.

Crimean Tatar identity: attempts at destruction

After the deportation, Crimea was overtaken by a wave of destruction of monuments to Crimean Tatar history and culture created by the Soviet authorities. Mosques and Muslim cemeteries were destroyed en masse. Russian ones replaced most toponyms of Crimean Tatar origin on the peninsula. Local flora and fauna were also severely affected: for example, some traditional grape varieties and two local dog breeds bred by Crimean Tatars disappeared. The greatest loss, however, was suffered by the Crimean Tatar language – a vital component of the national folk identity. Crimean Tatar literature was burned en masse in Crimea, and Crimean Tatar schools were completely liquidated. The language situation in exile was also bad: the working language was Russian in most schools, kindergartens and other educational institutions. In this situation, all hope rested on the family as the only source for transmitting the Crimean Tatar language and traditions. However, family opportunities were significantly minimized by mixed marriages and the general pressure to assimilate for mundane survival. As a result, UNESCO classified the Crimean Tatar language as *severely endangered.*

Life in exile

A large part of the Crimean Tatar population was deported to Uzbekistan to compact settlements under a special regime. The displaced were under surveillance by local authorities and experienced drastic restrictions on their own freedom of movement. They were allowed to leave the settlement only in exceptional cases, following requests from close relatives. In general, however, there was a strict ban on leaving the settlement: Violators could be fined, and if they violated it again, they could be imprisoned for up to 20 years.

In 1956, many Crimean Tatars were freed from "special settler" status and allowed to move within the Soviet Union. However, lifting restrictions did not provide for a return to their homeland, Crimea. The reason given was that Crimea was a completely inhabited region of Ukraine. This assertion, as well as pressure from the Soviet government to exterminate people of Crimean Tatar nationality in Uzbekistan, acted as a powerful catalyst for the activist groups, which gradually developed into a powerful Crimean Tatar national movement of significance throughout the Soviet Union. According to a decree passed in 1972, activists of the movement and virtually all Crimean Tatars who attempted to return to their homeland were declared "unreliable." This effectively legalized further reprisals, such as beatings, imprisonments, politically motivated prosecutions, etc., against activists. For restoring the rights and interests of their people, the Crimean Tatar population paid a high price – they were given the status of an "anti-Soviet element."

Return and integration

It was not until 1988 that the ban on resettling in Crimea was lifted. Only individual Crimean Tatar activists had nevertheless managed to return to Crimea before 1988.

> My parents were born in exile. Like me, they should have been born in Crimea, but in 1968, the year my parents were born, there were still no official opportunities to return. Only a small percentage of Crimean Tatars managed to return home earlier, despite the difficulties. These were basically active members of the Crimean Tatar national movement
>
> *Muslim, 26, from Kyiv, Ukraine.*

Even after the dream return to the homeland, times remained more than turbulent. The real estate that the Crimean Tatars had owned before the deportation had been confiscated by the state or occupied by new owners. As so-called compensation, the Soviet government provided empty and barren steppe areas in the north of Crimea, where the returnees had to try to somehow settle down without funds, gas, electricity and water. The most difficult challenge was the years-long struggle of people of Crimean Tatar ethnicity against Soviet propaganda.

Although the Crimean Tatar population was officially acquitted of all charges in 1967, the negative image of the Crimean Tatar people created by the Soviet Union remains so deeply rooted in society inside and outside Crimea that it continues to determine the fate of the Qirimli (the original name of the Crimean Tatars in Crimean Tatar) even decades later. One does not have to look for long for examples — it is enough to follow current news about the repressive measures of the occupying power against the Crimean Tatar population on the Crimean Peninsula illegally occupied by Russia.

Latent deportation in the 21st century

What has been happening to the Crimean Tatar people since the occupation of Crimea in 2014 is what many Ukrainian historians call latent deportation. Unfounded searches, mass arrests, politically motivated prosecutions, forced psychiatry, the murder of Reshat Ametov, and other violations of human rights — this is a Kremlin's response to the Crimean Tatars' aversion to the Russian occupation. Due to strong direct and indirect pressure, about 15,000 Crimean Tatars were forced to leave their homeland again indefinitely.

With the occupation of Crimea and all these repressive measures, Russia is joining the continuity of Soviet crimes committed before. It is hoped that the international community will not look the other way but openly name the injustice. Expulsion – including subversive expulsion – is and remains a crime against humanity.

Sources

Bekirova, Hulnara: "Deportaciya i borot'ba kryms'kyx tatar za povernennya na bat'kivshhynu (1944-1991)," *Independent Cultural Journal* Ї, 2018.

CrimeaSOS: "Deportation of Crimean Tatars. Crime told by witnesses." Part 1, 26.05.2016.

Hromenko, Serhii: "Vitchim narodiv. Navischo Stalin viseliv davni etnosi Krimu," ZN, UA, 19. 01. 2014.

Hromenko, Serhii: "S radyans'kyx mify pro kryms'kyx tatar. Dekonstrukciya," *Istorichna Pravda*, 18. 05. 2019.

Hallbach, Uwe: "Analysis: The Crimean Tatars in the Ukraine Crisis," Federal Agency for Civic Education, Bonn 2014.

Jobst, Kerstin: "Geschichte der Krim – Iphigenie und Putin auf Tauris," Walter de Gruyter Verlag, Berlin 2020.

Chapter 2

Occupation Forces in the Second World War

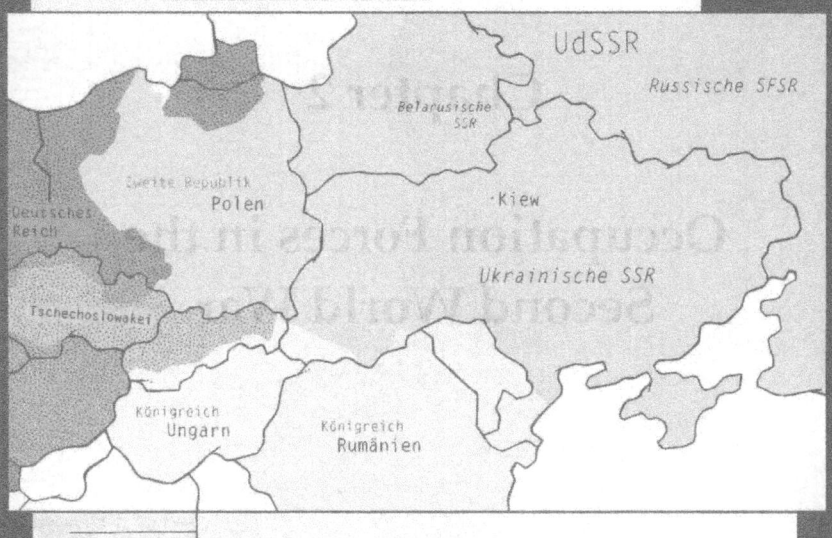

Moskau, den 23. August 1939

The Legacy of the Hitler-Stalin Pact
Ukraine between Nation and Imperial Rule

Jan Claus Behrends

The pact between Stalin's Soviet Union and Nazi Germany, concluded in Moscow in August 1939, continues to cause political tension and historical controversy today. The alliance of dictators stands at the beginning of the Second World War, which began with the joint aggression of Germany and the Soviet Union against Poland and the division of Eastern Europe into imperial spheres of influence, recorded in the secret Supplementary Protocol. Thus, Stalin's USSR and the Third Reich jointly destroyed the nation-state order that had emerged since 1917 as a consequence of the defeat of the imperial powers in Eastern Europe. Only 20 years after the end of World War I, the revanchist powers had gained the upper hand. Poland and the Baltic States paid for the German-Soviet alliance with their sovereignty. Eastern Europe was at the mercy of two imperial powers, and both were modern dictatorships.

For several decades, the Soviet government denied the consequences of the Hitler-Stalin Pact. Only Mikhail Gorbachev and Boris Yeltsin slowly acknowledged the historical reality. However, under Vladimir Putin, there was a rollback in historical policy: in recent years, Russia has persistently tried to relativize and normalize the August 23, 1939, treaty. One Kremlin strategy seizes on the Soviet argument that Moscow was forced to sign the pact for security reasons. The other argument is based on the claim that the pact was a treaty like any other. Other states, such as Poland in 1934 or Great Britain in 1935, had also signed treaties with Hitler. These arguments are incorrect since the crucial component of the Pact was the secret Additional Protocol, which turned the official "non-aggression pact" not only into an alliance but de facto into a pact of aggression against Poland and the Baltic States. Warsaw and the Baltic States, whose peoples in August 1989 made an impressive human chain to point out the historical injustice of the pact, therefore rightly oppose the Putin regime's attempts to deny the German-Soviet entente of 1939. For the Kremlin, on the other hand, at stake is the narrative of the "Great Patriotic War" and the "liberation of Europe" that legitimized the Soviet Union before 1991 and Russian statehood today.

The focus on Russia, Poland, the Baltic States and the beginning of the war on September 1, 1939, obscures the fact that countries such as Romania, Ukraine, Belarus and Moldova have also been affected by the consequences of the Hitler-Stalin Pact to this day. This is particularly true of Ukraine, whose present-day shape is a direct consequence of the 1939 caesura.

Unlike Poland, Ukraine had not succeeded in asserting its short-lived independence in the Russian Civil War after the collapse of the Tsarist Empire. Galicia went to Poland in the 1921 Peace of Riga, and eastern Ukraine became a Soviet republic. Ukrainians thus lived in the interwar period either as a minority in the Polish nation-state or as a titular nation in the Soviet Union, where political decisions were made in Moscow and not in Ukraine. As early as the 1920s, the Soviet leadership tried to use the Ukrainian minority in Poland to destabilize the neighboring country. Developments in the Soviet Union were far more dramatic than in Piłsudksi's Poland: The brief flowering of Ukrainian culture through the nationalities policy of the early Soviet Union was followed not only by Russification under Stalin but also by the Holodomor in 1932/33 as a result of collectivization and the "Great Terror" of 1937/38. Despite all the propaganda, the radiance of Soviet Ukraine on the diaspora in Poland, therefore, remained limited. The hardship, misery and oppression in the Soviet constituent republic were too great. Nevertheless, the Ukrainians in Galicia were also discriminated against: as a national minority, they were tolerated, but they stood on the fringes of society.

Ukraine, which did not yet exist as an independent state in 1939, is nevertheless shaped by the decisions of that year to the present day. Although the annexation of Galicia was only one episode in the decades of terror and violence (1905–1953), the Sovietization of western Ukraine during 1939–1941 set a decisive course for the entire country. On September 17, 1939, Soviet troops crossed the border, stabbing the Polish army, who were fighting the Wehrmacht, in the back. The justification for the invasion was not the revolutionary uprising against the "Polish Pane" but the national liberation of Ukraine: It was the task of the Red Army, as the daily order stated, to prevent the further "enslavement" of the "White Russian and Ukrainian brothers." Stalin's propagandist Yemelyan Yaroslavsky wrote in *Pravda* that it was a matter of "helping the like-blooded [*edinokrovniy*] Ukrainians and Belarusians living in Poland." The Soviet justification for the invasion was in line with the folk thinking of the era.

After the revolutions of 1905 and 1917, the Civil War and the Holodomor, another phase of mass violence began in 1939/40 on the soil of what is now Ukraine. The Sovietization of western Ukraine was simultaneously an ethnic cleansing that affected primarily, but by no means exclusively, the Polish population. The Polish state was crushed, and its representatives lost their offices, property, and often their freedom or lives. Thus, in the autumn of 1939, the Ukrainization of these ethnically mixed territories began. The German invasion of the Soviet Union in the summer of 1941 escalated the violence again—to the genocide of the Jewish population under German occupation. In his study of the small Galician town of Buczacz (formerly Buchach), Omer Bartov described how this combination of Sovietization, occupation, Shoah, and, since 1944, renewed Sovietization shaped an entirely new society. That multiethnicity that had characterized Ukraine for centuries was lost due to the mass murders, expulsion, discrimination, and deportation of minorities in large parts of the country. The cities of Ukraine were repopulated. For a long time, the experience of extermination and genocide was burned into the memory of the survivors.

The geopolitical realities created in August 1939 endured after the defeat of Germany. Stalin retained the eastern Polish territories (the *kresy*) and the Baltic States as part of the USSR. Thus, post-war Ukraine consisted of a larger eastern part, which had already belonged to the Soviet Union since 1922, and the Galician west, where, despite all the disasters, the legacy of the Austro-Hungarian era and the Polish period remained visible. Similar to the Baltic region in the north, Galicia was, therefore, in many respects more "European" than the rest of the USSR and was perceived as such. There was a cultural difference between the parts of the country that had suffered the Holodomor and the terror of the 1930s and the areas that had been part of the USSR only since 1939 (with the interruption of the German occupation). The border between the Soviet and the East-Central European experience of communism runs through Ukraine. In this respect, the country differs from Russia, the Caucasian states or central Asia.

At least as dramatic as the war and mass violence that followed the Hitler-Stalin Pact is the deeper geopolitical question that was decided differently in 1918, 1939, 1945 and 1989: Should Eastern Europe, like the west of the continent, be characterized by nation-states, or is it an imperially dominated space in which only great powers are truly sovereign?

The year 1939 marked the return to the imperial order after only two decades, which only collapsed a second time in the wake of the upheaval of 1989/91. With the wars against Georgia in 2008 and against Ukraine since 2014, the Kremlin has shown that it is once again prepared to use military force to enforce its imperial ambitions. As in the fall of 1939, the supposed protection of threatened minorities is again used as an argument to legitimize an intervention in foreign states. This continuity of imperial thinking and action currently threatens peace in Europe.

In 1939, Poland was the victim of an imperial rollback; since 2014, it is now Ukraine. Unlike the world eighty years ago, Moscow's imperial thinking in the present leads to isolation. In Europe, the Kremlin stands alone. Nevertheless, Vladimir Putin's pursuit of hegemony and his determination to use military force is a reality that Europeans must confront once again. The geopolitical order in the east of the continent remains fragile.

Ukraine Under Nazi Rule

Karel C. Berkhoff

Ukraine was very important in Nazi plans, for it belonged to the *Lebensraum* (living space) that the Germans supposedly needed in order to survive. Ukraine's fertile lands would enable them to revitalize their agrarian roots and thus regenerate themselves as a Germanic "race". Moreover, the produce from there would foster the Third Reich's economic independence. Except for the ethnic Germans, not just Jews but the entire native population, sooner or later, would have to be removed from an "East" where ultimately only people of "pure German blood" would live. What was the result of an invasion driven by such an ideology?

At the time of the German invasion that began on 22, June 1941, the Soviet Union had recently expanded the Ukrainian Soviet Socialist Republic through annexation from Poland and Romania of western Volhynia, eastern Galicia, northern Bukovina, and southern Bessarabia. After an initial period of military rule, the largest German territorial unit became the Reichskommissariat Ukraine, headquartered in Rivne and led by Reich Commissar Erich Koch. It had five large districts: Volhynia-Podolia, Zhytomyr, Kyiv, Mykolaiv, Dnipropetrovsk, and a "partial district" called Taurida. In the north, the Reichskommissariat included regions that today are part of Belarus. Meanwhile, the city of Lviv and the rest of eastern Galicia was made part of the Galicia District within a German territory called the Generalgouvernement Polen (Government General). The Galicia District was subdivided into counties and under Governor Karl Lasch and then Otto Wächter. Germany's Rear Army Area South, in the far eastern military zone of occupation, was ruled by Karl von Roques and Erich Friderici. Finally, Subcarpathian Rus', or Transcarpathia, continued to be ruled by Hungary, which had annexed it in 1939.

Life and death under Nazi rule were brutal and full of fear. Terror took many forms: plunder; evictions from homes; deportations; and above all, the mass murder of Jews, Roma, psychiatric patients, prisoners of war, Communists, Soviet activists, and other suspects. The killings were often carried out for everyone to see. A wide range of German "security" units amply used their unbridled license to kill. These units included commandos of two large task forces of the Security Police and Security Service, the Einsatzgruppe C and Einsatzgruppe D. But besides these mobile killing squads, later turned into local offices of the Security Police and Security Service, there were also nine battalions of the regular German Order Police, the 1st SS Infantry Brigade of the Waffen-SS, and three army security divisions. Numerous camps were created, such as Syrets in Kyiv and Janowska in Lviv.

Never before in the history of Ukraine, with the time of the Great Famine of 1933 as a possible exception, did so many social and ethnic groups suffer so much during one period. For most of inhabitants of the new Reichskommissariat Ukraine, conditions were far worse than anywhere in western Europe, and also far worse than in the Generalgouvernement. That said, Galicia was also littered with new corpses and mass graves. So was Rear Army Area South, to which the Donbas (Donets Basin) and Crimea belonged and which did not have a German civilian administration. In fact, no military occupation regime in European history had ever been as brutal as this one. The German armed forces in the military zone of occupation were responsible for mass crimes, mainly because the Wehrmacht had become thoroughly nazified and its leaders largely shared Hitler's views on Jews and Slavs.

Two southern Ukrainian regions were fully rejoined with the Romanian state: northern Bukovina (with Chernivtsi) and the Bessabarian south of the current Odesa oblast. Other southwestern Ukrainian regions between the Southern Buh and Dniester rivers, including the city of Odesa, became part of Transnistria. Formally separate from the Romanian state, this entity had thirteen districts or counties and a governor, Gheorghe Alexianu. Transnistria had about two hundred ghettos, concentration camps, and penal labor camps. The most lethal of these, where Romanians and Ukrainian and ethnic German policemen carried out mass shootings of Jews, were in the Holta district at Akhmechetka, Bohdanivka, and Domanivka.

Jews, Roma, and psychiatric patients

The victims of Nazi murder were mainly Jews, Roma, psychiatric patients, and prisoners of war. On the eve of the Second World War, about five percent of Soviet Ukraine's population was of Jewish descent. By the middle of 1941, there were about 2.7 million Jews within present-day Ukraine's borders (those internationally recognized as of 2016). During the German-led war against the Soviet Union, a stunning proportion of them, some 1.5 million, died at the hands of Germans as well as Romanians, Hungarians, Ukrainians, and others. About 60 percent of the pre-war Jewish population was murdered. Some 900,000 Jews had fled or were evacuated to the east in time, mostly from the industrialized eastern Dnieper bend and the Donbas. But in Ukraine's western regions, the Jewish communities of Galicia, Volhynia, and Podolia were exterminated almost in full. In eastern Galicia, just a few percent of the Jews survived; in Volhynia, even less. Overall, only about 100,000 Jews survived in Ukraine while it was under Nazi rule.

Soon after the invasion that began in late June 1941, ever greater proportions of Jews were murdered. This process included able-bodied men (early July); Jews among the prisoners of war (middle of July); and then also women and children (late August). Although some individual SS officers had begun shooting Jewish women and children, the expansion of the shootings was driven from the top, mainly by the Higher SS and Police Leader Russia South, Friedrich Jeckeln. It is a little known fact that Romania initially acted even more radically. Hence, from the very start, while Germans were focusing on Jewish men, in little-known Bukovinian and Bessarabian places the Romanian invaders shot not only Jewish men but also women and children.

Pogroms may be defined as spontaneous or seemingly spontaneous acts of anti-Jewish violence by locals. They erupted in June and July 1941, soon after the start of the German invasion, in regions of western Ukraine that less than two years before had recently been occupied by the Soviet Union. Thousands of Jews were killed in pogroms in numerous localities, including the cities of Lviv and Ternopil. Principal responsibility remained with the invaders, who wanted and encouraged such pogroms. Nevertheless, radical Ukrainian nationalists were involved, if only because of their own propaganda. For instance, when Germans occupied Lviv on June 30, 1941, supporters of Stepan Bandera's Organization of Ukrainian Nationalists told the people in a proclamation that "Moscow, Poland, the Hungarians, the Jews are your enemies. Destroy them." The next day, a pogrom by all kinds of perpetrators began and climaxed in the German shooting of hundreds of Jews.

After the pogroms, there were in Ukraine some two thousand German murder actions that took the form of shootings of large and small groups of Jews. The transition toward mass shootings took place at a breathtaking speed. An important watershed event, which established that Germans would murder entire Jewish communities, was the mass shooting of 23,600 Jews in Kamianets-Podilskyi, a town near the pre-1939 border between Poland and Romania.

Kyiv became the first large city anywhere in Europe where virtually all its Jewish inhabitants were murdered in one stroke, mainly on 29 and 30 September 1941. Less than a week later, mines that were deliberately placed by the departing NKVD and Red Army engineers exploded, setting off a fire that demolished most of the city center. Analogously, the Romanian occupiers killed about 25,000 of the about 90,000 Jews in Odesa in two days in October 1941, after a Soviet mine there killed a Romanian general and sixty officers and soldiers.

In the second half of 1942, a second and final wave of mass shootings began and moved from eastern to western Ukraine, murdering the remaining Jews. Here eastern Galicia stood out in the sense that mass shootings also occurred there late in the war and that its Jews were also deported and gassed in the death camp of Bełżec.

Ukraine had Jewish ghettos, places where Jews were concentrated with restrictions on entry and departure. Mostly existing in eastern Galicia and Volhynia, and mostly set up by the German

Army, they were meant to fully isolate and then kill the inmates. Besides the ghettos there were numerous forced labor camps; those around Transit Highway 4 first held local Jews and then Jewish deportees from Transnistria.

Growing international awareness of the shootings and the diminishing prospects for a German victory in the war prompted a Nazi effort to destroy the evidence; that is the corpses of the dead. A Special Commando 1005 forced prisoners to unearth the mass graves with the Jewish (and non-Jewish) victims.

Ukraine's Roma were also exterminated for racist reasons. Little is known about that history, which largely remains to be written. In southern Ukraine, including Crimea, sedentary Roma were shot already from the fall of 1941, without differentiating them from the so-called itinerant Gyspsies being killed by the Nazis in other regions. Merging of the treatment of all Roma with that of the Jews was the personal initiative of Otto Ohlendorf, the leader of Einsatzgruppe D.

Psychiatric patients were also systematically murdered. In Kyiv, for instance, starting with the Jews among them, almost eight hundred were shot or gassed in four waves, and buried in or near Babyn Yar.

Prisoners of war

The other large group killed in the German massacres were the Soviet prisoners of war, a term which can be misleading. Some of these prisoners did not consider themselves "Soviet," and they actually included many who were not formally soldiers but NKVD troops, the People's Levy, railroad workers, and civilians building fortifications.

French, British, American, and Canadian military men in German captivity, even if they were of Jewish descent, were very likely to survive World War II. In stark contrast, between 2.8 and 3 million persons considered to be Soviet POWs died in German captivity in Ukraine and beyond, and about a third did so while near the frontline. (The number specifically for Ukraine is difficult to establish.)

Almost always, Jews among the prisoners were immediately shot. Meanwhile, from the Nazi perspective, the inferior Slavs could be useful. That was why POWs identified as Ukrainian often were released, especially in 1941. Unofficial Ukrainian Red Cross societies played an important role in these releases. But many soldiers in the Wehrmacht evidently assumed that Bolshevism, the vicious ideology and political party supposedly created by "Jewry," had irreversibly "infected" all soldiers whom they called Russian, regardless of their actual ethnic background. In this nazified frame of mind, such "Russians" were either superfluous or positively dangerous.

Therefore, not only guidelines and orders — such as the "Commissar Order," a death verdict on military commissars issued even before the invasion — but also racism created an unmistakable scenario: the deliberate destruction of most of the POWs. The starvation, abuse, and shooting of the "Russian" POWs was not solely due to racism. But that factor did make it possible to embark on the abuse and murder in the first place.

After initial shootings, the prisoners were marched westward via transit camps toward permanent camps, often for very long distances. These are best described as death marches, for German (and Hungarian) army escorts shot on sight fugitives and stragglers, and mostly prevented locals from giving the prisoners food or water. Because the harvest of 1941 was excellent, the German authorities and the native population had plenty of food to spare. The latter tried hard to pass some of it on but German policy makers wanted most of the prisoners to die, and so they deliberately starved the numerous POWs who could not work. Feeding non-working POWs was even proclaimed "wrongheaded humanity." Camp guards often shot at civilians who tried to save lives. Had those civilians not been obstructed so much, and had the escorts and camp guards behaved in a more humane fashion, hundreds of thousands of lives could and would have been saved.

Unless prisoners got out through release or escape, their only chance for survival was to be selected for daytime work outside the camp. Flight attempts by Soviet POWs were a daily event, whether during the marches, in the camps, and at the work sites. The escapes were often facilitated by outsiders.

Peasants and city dwellers

Peasants who had not been members of a Soviet collective farm had to join its German successor, the "communal" farm, and all members had to actually work there, even — unlike before 1941 — the women with small children. Regulations on the duration of that labor became more and more strict. Machine-Tractor Stations often became bases for supervision of the farms. The supervisors — Germans, Dutch, and apparently also natives — tended to be ruthless and to force peasants to work even on important holidays. Worst of all, Germans abused the peasants for the smallest things, such as not saying a proper greeting, failing to do so at once, or having one's hands in one's pockets.

Many peasants had on average more food at their disposal in the two to three years of German rule than they used to have under Soviet rule, mainly because they worked their gardens well and because for a long time the German system of supervision and requisition was less efficient than its Soviet predecessor. But the main problem for the peasants was that collective farming remained and eventually became what they considered full-blown serfdom. The ever-increasing abuse and violence were why, eventually, most peasants feared for their lives whenever a German was around. Moreover, girls and women knew they could be arrested and locked up somewhere in an army brothel.

Terror and food shortages were the key elements of everyday city life. In the cities, passers-by could be forced to watch public hangings of those labeled saboteurs or Jews. Inhabitants of large cities also saw gas vans speeding by. They called them mobile gas-chambers, each of which could hold fifty prisoners. They were the *dushehubka* — destroyers of the soul. Shots resounded from many killing sites down to the very end of Nazi rule. And that included Babyn Yar. City dwellers also constantly encountered overt racism. Germans never stood in line and always could claim a seat in trams. There came insults ("Russian pig!") and widespread and official physical abuse, even for misunderstanding something. Making ends meet was hard, particularly for intellectuals. For instance, in early 1942, all institutes of higher education in the Reichskommissariat were closed.

In the winter of 1941–1942, there was a major famine in Crimea, in which hundreds, if not thousands, of civilians and prisoners of war starved to death. In Kyiv and Kharkiv, meanwhile, large numbers starved to death in *artificial* famines deliberately created by the German authorities in order to get rid of human beings considered useless or dangerous. There was plenty of food around these cities, even late in 1941; consequently, peasants were eager to barter with the proceeds of their rich harvest. But police cordons were set up with the express purpose of confiscating "surplus" food. Everything was confiscated unless a large bribe was paid. If not, peasants and city dwellers were blocked from venturing into or out of urban centers. In July 1942, for instance, General Commissar Waldemar Magunia banned "free" or "illicit" food trade in Kyiv. Although the blockades were not total, they nonetheless cost many lives.

Ten thousand may approach the number of famine deaths in Kyiv. But famine was not the only reason for the drop in the city's population in less than two years, from an estimated 400,000 in October to 300,000 in 1943. Flight, deportation to Germany, and Nazi shootings also played their part in the precipitous drop of numbers.

For a long time, the frontline remained only fifty kilometers away from the eastern city of Kharkiv. Although it was the largest Soviet city ever occupied by the Germans, the number of inhabitants was less than 500,000. While the Germans ruled Kharkiv from October 1941 to August 1943 (except for four weeks early in 1943), the city commander demanded "extreme harshness" toward the locals and he had, as he wrote to other Germans, "no interest whatsoever" in feeding them.

At least 30,000 Kharkivans starved to death. This figure is the minimum because of unclarity about the famine deaths far beyond the city: emaciated Kharkivans who were deported and died from exhaustion on their way to the Reich, or soon after arriving there. It is clear, however, that in no other city in Europe occupied by the

German armed forces did so many who were not Jewish suffer and die from famine.

Deportations to Germany

Early in 1942, in the wake of many mass shootings of Ukraine's Jews and Roma and a winter of hunger for prisoners and city-dwellers, the German authorities launched a campaign to obtain laborers for factories and farms in the Reich. They had not anticipated such a campaign before the war, but now felt the need to alleviate the unexpected labor shortages in Greater Germany. Some financial assistance was provided to the family members of the Ostarbeiter (Eastern Workers), as they were called in the Reich. After news about the bad working conditions in Germany spread, many Ukrainians became terrified of being sent there. In order to be disqualified, many people in Ukraine mutilated themselves. Some were convinced that they would die in Germany, whether from famine or Allied bombs. They also started to doubt that Germans were only murdering Jews and Roma. Contemporary songs and sayings about the deportations expressed profound sadness.

When there were no more volunteers, the Germans sent out commissions to carry out the deportations. Local administrators in Ukraine were threatened with death if they could not supply the assigned total of "recruits." Sometime in late 1942, native officials no longer had to supply a certain number of people, but simply all people of a certain age. Hence, it was not just German policemen, but raion leaders, city mayors, and auxiliary policemen who started to arrest people for deportation. Round-ups became a frequent phenomenon at city markets. Those who tried to escape were shot at. In the countryside, the police simply went from house to house.

Still frustrated, the regime took even harsher action, ordering for instance, in the Volhynia-Podolia General District, the burning of the homes of those who refused to go, and confining relatives to labor camps as hostages. Entire villages went up in flames. The boarding of the deportation trains also produced highly violent and emotional scenes. Soon more and more auxiliary policemen, realizing that Germany was losing the war, began issuing warnings of upcoming round-ups, and sometimes helping people to escape.

One in every forty inhabitants of the Reichskommissariat and Rear Army Area South combined was deported by August 1943. Ultimately, 1,500,000 people from these two Ukrainian regions ended up in Germany's Third Reich. They were mostly villages, but ultimately the deportations affected almost every family in Ukraine.

Auxiliaries

Particularly in the Reichskommissariat, the "Ukrainian auxiliary administration," as it was collectively called, consisted of city administrations each headed by a mayor, raion administrations each headed by a raion chief, and village administrations each headed by a village elder (starosta). These figures played an important role in Nazi rule, if only because the invader initially lacked detailed knowledge of local affairs. But there was no one body representing the Ukrainian populace as a whole. In that sense, Ukrainians in Galicia were better off, having a local branch of the Cracow-based Ukrainian Central Committee, led by Volodymyr Kubijovyč.

The earliest local police formations, particularly in western Ukraine, appeared as militias with little or no German involvement right after the invasion started. After a while the Einsatzgruppen or the German military reduced the size of these militias, not least by expelling many OUN members. In the Reichskommissariat alone, there were eventually about 80,000 police auxiliaries — four times as many as German policemen.

The police auxiliaries played a key role in intimidating, abusing, robbing, arresting, guarding, and sometimes even personally murdering Jews. They also transported Jews from the countryside to major cities for questioning, which was generally followed by murder. Wherever ghettos were formed, these policemen tended to plunder and guard them. The sad climax of their participation in the Holocaust came during the second half of 1942, when they drove the victims and stood guard at the shooting pits.

The level of involvement in these actions of the Organization of Ukrainian Nationalists, be it the faction led by Stepan Bandera (OUN-B) or the faction led by Andrii Melnyk (OUN-M), remains problematic and is far from a "case closed." A good example is the large Bukovinian Battalion. This unit was comprised of thousands of Ukrainians of the OUN Melnyk faction, which in early August 1941 left Bukovina for Kyiv and elsewhere in Ukraine. Some writers say that they have established beyond doubt that the men and women of the Bukovinian Battalion were not in Kyiv during the Babyn Yar massacre—and therefore could have been involved in it in any way. On the other hand, some Ukrainian emigrés (among them Yaroslav Haivas) have recalled that thousands of nationalists were in nearby Zhytomyr for an important funeral in late August 1941, and that "as soon as Kyiv was liberated from the Bolsheviks, everyone wanted to be there and at once. They were unstoppable." Indeed, Bukovinians did arrive in Kyiv while the Khreshchatyk "was burning," and one Jewish survivor (Viktor Stadnik) recalled seeing them in the city center in September. The question, then, is whether one can rule out the arrival of all of the Bukovinians in that month.

The relationship between the Germans and the Ukrainian nationalist activists deteriorated quickly. First, in the summer of 1941, the OUN-B began to be persecuted, mainly because that faction refused to annul its declaration of Ukrainian statehood made in Lviv on the day (June 30, 1941) that the German Army arrived in the city. The OUN-M, which was particularly active in Kyiv, was suppressed as well. Nevertheless, it generally remained open to the possibility of collaboration with Germany.

Partisans

The OUN-B mostly broke with Germany in early 1943, in particular after it set up in central and southern Volhynia a large Ukrainian Insurgent Army (UPA). Historians generally agree that, like so many other partisan forces in Europe during World War II, the UPA perpetrated massacres of innocent civilians, in this case mainly Poles. The Soviet partisans also made a big impact on everyday life. They engaged in sabotage and they distributed leaflets and newspapers, but at least as high on their agenda was killing, and not just of Germans. Ukraine's NKVD had as its official goal systematically to "exterminate" the "fascist" regime that was set up in Ukraine. The Soviet partisans seemingly paid little or no attention to the consequences of their actions for locals.

The predominant German reaction to partisan activity was to kill and burn, with careful planning and horrible precision, some 50,000 people. This often happened in the wake of village burnings, especially in northern Ukraine, where sustained partisan activity was made possible by protection from the abundance of forests. Nevertheless, the Germans destroyed over three hundred villages fully or in part. One of the earliest casualties of these assaults in the Reichskommissariat became the village of Kortelisy near Ratne in the Polissia region. On 23 September 1943, auxiliary policemen and a German police company based in Brest-Litovsk (with mainly policemen from Nuremberg) surrounded the village. After ordering everyone, including all the children, to assemble, they shot nearly 2,900 inhabitants with submachine guns and pistols, or drowned them, or bayonetted them to death.

In February 1943, Soviet partisans led by Oleksii Fedorov attacked the garrison in the small town of Koriukivka in the Chernihiv region, in an attempt to liberate hostages. The garrison consisted of German soldiers, Hungarians, and auxiliary policemen. In the terrible revenge that followed, on 1 and 2 March, the entire town was annihilated. Survivors were finished off on 9 March. Koriukivka had become an ash heap filled with the remains of thousands of people. This was just one group among the many who lost their lives as direct or indirect result of the Nazi occupation of Ukraine.

Further reading

Amar, Tarik Cyril. *The Paradox of Ukrainian Lviv: A Borderland City between Stalinists, Nazis, and Nationalists.* Ithaca, NY: Cornell University Press, 2015.

Angrick, Andrej. *Besatzungspolitik und Massenmord: die Einsatzgruppe D in der südlichen Sowjetunion 1941–1943.* Hamburg: Hamburger Edition, 2003.

Berkhoff, Karel C. *Harvest of Despair: Life and Death in Ukraine under Nazi Rule.* Cambridge, Massachusetts: The Belknap Press of Harvard University Press, 2004.

Berkhoff, Karel. "The Holocaust in Ukraine." EHRI Online Course in Holocaust Studies, European Holocaust Research Infrastructure. http://training.ehri-project.eu/unit/3-holocaust-ukraine .

Dereiko, Ivan. *Mistsevi formuvannia nimets'koï armiï ta politsiï u Raikhskomisariati "Ukraïna" (1941–1944 roky).* Kyiv: Instytut istoriï Ukraïny NAN Ukraïny, 2012.

Gogun, Alexander. *Stalin's Commandos: Ukrainian Partisan Forces on the Eastern Front.* London: I. B. Tauris, 2015.

Il'iushyn, Ihor. *Ukraïns'ka Povstans'ka Armiia i Armiia Kraiova: protystoiannia v Zakhidnii Ukraïni (1939–1945 rr.).* Kyiv: Kyievo-Mohylians'ka akademiia, 2009.

Lower, Wendy. *Nazi Empire-Building and the Holocaust in Ukraine.* Chapel Hill, N.C.: University of North Carolina Press, 2005.

Malakov, Dmytro. *Oti dva roky…: u Kyievi pry nimtsiakh.* Kyiv: Amadei, 2002.

Mick, Christoph. *Lemberg, Lwów, L'viv, 1914–1947: Violence and Ethnicity in a Contested City.* West Lafayette, Ind.: Purdue University Press, 2015.

Patryliak, I. K. and Boryvyk, M. A. *Ukraïna v roky Druhoï svitovoï viiny: sproba novoho kontseptual'noho pohliadu.* Nizhyn: PP Lysenko M. M., 2010

Penter, Tanja. *Kohle für Stalin und Hitler: arbeiten und Leben im Donbass 1929 bis 1953.* Essen: Klartext Verlag, 2010.

Pohl, Dieter. *Die Herrschaft der Wehrmacht: deutsche Militärbesatzung und einheimische Bevölkerung in der Sowjetunion 1941–1944.* Munich: R. Oldenbourg Verlag, 2008.

Rossoliński-Liebe, Grzegorz. *Stepan Bandera: The Life and Afterlife of a Ukrainian Nationalist. Fascism, Genocide, and Cult.* Stuttgart and Hannover: Ibidem, 2014.

Skorobohatov, A. V. *Kharkiv u chasy nimets'koï okupatsiï (1941–1943).* Kharkiv: Prapor, 2004.

Struve, Kai. *Deutsche Herrschaft, ukrainischer Nationalismus, antijüdische Gewalt: Der Sommer 1941 in der Westukraine.* Munich: De Gruyter Oldenbourg, 2015.

Stepan Bandera
On the Historical and Political Background of a Symbolic Figure

Wilfried Jilge

One of the central theses of Russian historical propaganda in the Ukraine crisis is that the *banderovtsy*, that is, Russophobic radical nationalists, anti-Semites, or "radical neo-Nazi groups" such as the "Right Sector" and the radical nationalist party *Svoboda* were the decisive forces behind the protests on the Maidan; they brought about the change of power in Kyiv in a fascist coup during February 21–22, 2014. As a factor in the Maidan's self-defense, the "Right Sector" indeed played a role during the violent final phase of the Maidan protests, and *Svoboda* was represented as the smallest party in the alliance of the parliamentary opposition. However, they never dominated the agenda of the protests and had no chance in the presidential and parliamentary elections. The effect of the stereotype of the *banderovtsy* on the Russian public owes much to the presence of the Soviet myth of the "Great Patriotic War" in the politics of history and the culture of memory in contemporary Russia. It forms one of the central elements of the patriotism that Russian President Putin propagated. In the propagandistically used Soviet war history image, the *banderovtsy* were among the main enemies of the Soviet state.

Ukrainian politician Stepan Bandera headed the Organization of Ukrainian Nationalists (OUN), split in 1940, which resisted the Soviet occupation of western Ukraine during World War II and co-operated with Nazi Germany at various periods. In the Soviet view of history, Bandera and the OUN are associated primarily with crimes and terror against the "peaceful Soviet population" and presented as mere puppets of the Germans. On this basis, state-directed Russian media make an analogy between the invasion of the German Wehrmacht in the summer of 1941 and the protests on the Kyiv Maidan: from this perspective, the "new banderovtsy" in Kyiv are collaborators of the US and the European Union who turn against Russian-speaking people and against everything Russian in general.

However, the stereotype of the *banderovtsy* fulfills a much more important function: it is intended to discredit the independent Ukrainian nation and the European integration it seeks in free self-determination. To this end, the popular science monographs published in Russia in 2014 about Bandera and Russian-Ukrainian relations resort to a slightly modified interpretation of the 1654 Treaty of Pereiaslav.

In 1648, the uprising of the Ukrainian Cossacks against the Polish aristocracy began. Their hard-pressed leader, the hetman Bohdan Khmelnytsky (ca. 1595–1657), finally turned to the tsar with a request for help in securing the autonomy of the Cossack statehood he had established since 1648/49. In 1654, an assembly of Cossacks in Pereiaslav declared themselves in favor of subordination to the tsar and swore an oath of allegiance to him. The interpretation of the Treaty of Pereiaslav remains controversial to this day. Some Ukrainian historians emphasize that it was a terminable military alliance of two states based on equality. On the other hand, Russian historians usually understand the treaty as the incorporation of Ukraine into the Moscow Empire.

While in the national Ukrainian historical image, the era of Khmelnytskyi's Cossack statehood is regarded as the golden age and an expression of Ukrainian independence, for the Soviet historiography relevant here, Pereiaslav is the symbol of the "reunification of Ukraine with Russia," which was then finally consolidated in the "Great Patriotic War." In 1954, as part of the elaborately staged, month-long state celebrations marking the 300th anniversary of the treaty, the Crimean Peninsula was incorporated into the Ukrainian Soviet Republic. Pereiaslav was celebrated as a symbol of the unbreakable friendship of Ukrainians and Russians and as a sign of the regained unity of the East Slavic peoples (Russians, Ukrainians, Belarusians) after the disintegration of Kyiv Rus, the end of the supposedly unified "Old Russian nationhood."

Suppose before 1991, the myth of Pereiaslav cemented the affiliation of Ukrainians to the Soviet Union alongside the "big

Russian brother" today. In that case, the argumentation in Russian historical policy serves the idea of Russians and Ukrainians as "brothers in blood and faith" and the legitimization of a "natural" integration into the "Russian world" [russkij mir] led by Russia. In this sense, a recent Russian book on Stepan Bandera states that there are "two Ukraines": A "real Ukraine, the Ukraine of the Council of Pereiaslav [...] and the Slavic brotherhood, which is united with Russia," and a "pro-Western, Russophobic Ukraine," "with which we had to fight not only once in the past." Moreover, the author continues, "the banderovtsy hold on to power, it is not impossible that in the future you will have to fight again."

Indeed, the OUN and its wing, led by Stepan Bandera, were involved in crimes. However, they were by no means pure puppets of the Germans: their primary goal was always establishing a Ukrainian state, which ultimately ran counter to German goals. That the ultra-nationalist ideology of the OUN cannot be equated *a priori* with German National Socialism is shown by a look at its history.

The founding of the OUN in Vienna in 1929 was also an attempt by the Ukrainian representatives of a "new nationalism" to draw the right conclusions from the failed attempts at Ukrainian state-building from 1917 to 1921. Among these "new nationalists" was Dmytro Dontsov (1883–1973), a native of eastern Ukraine, who — without being a formal member of the organization — became the most important ideologist and mastermind of the OUN's radical "integral nationalism" in the 1920s. Dontsov and his followers concluded that Ukrainians did not yet constitute a nation but an "amorphous mass" incapable of exercising rule. Therefore, the goal was not to liberate a nation but to create one in the first place. In the sense of Dontsov's voluntarism, nation-building had to be accomplished by the will and the "masculine-heroic" deed of a nationalist elite. In this way, Dontsov turned against "weak liberalism" and laid the foundations for the OUN's anti-democratic, anti-parliamentary and authoritarian ideology and its hierarchical structure, which was strictly based on the leader principle. The OUN rejected the party system and saw itself as a non-partisan movement in which the different political forces of Ukrainians should gather.

However, the latter failed because of the OUN's absolute claim to power: Thus, none of the legalistic parties of Ukrainians in Poland (where most Ukrainians lived outside Soviet Ukraine) wanted to subordinate themselves to the leadership of the OUN.

The OUN's "integral nationalism" was initially closely modeled on Italian fascism. Its most important political goal was establishing an authoritarian and professionally structured Ukrainian state. All other goals were subordinated to the goal of statehood.

The members of the OUN saw themselves as the avant-garde, whose cadres were to educate Ukrainians to become a nation based on their own state. The protagonists of the OUN saw war as the only way to liberation and state independence. A peaceful fulfillment of the Ukrainian aspiration for independence within the power constellation and peace order that prevailed in Europe during the interwar period was inconceivable.

The main principles of "integral nationalism" were summarized in the *Ten Commandments of the Ukrainian Nationalists*, the so-called *Decalogue*. Radical national egoism and ruthlessness towards the enemies of the Ukrainian nation and its future state formed the basis. The *Decalogue* demanded unconditional sacrifice from every Ukrainian nationalist. This included violent struggle, without which, in the OUN's view, a Ukrainian state could not be achieved. In this way, individual terror and crimes could be morally justified if they served the interests of the Ukrainian nation.

In the southeastern areas of Poland inhabited by Ukrainians, the OUN built up a strong underground organization in the 1930s. Beginning in 1930, it fought against Polish rule with acts of terror and sabotage. Tadeusz Hołówko, one of the few Polish politicians who stood up for the rights of the Ukrainian minority, also fell victim to the assassinations. The OUN's terror was directed primarily, but not exclusively, against the Polish state and its representatives. It also targeted, for example, moderate Ukrainians, (Ukrainian) communists, and a representative of Soviet institutions in Poland. The Polish state reacted, among other things, with a brutal "pacification" of Ukrainian villages. The political development of Ukrainians in Poland must also be seen in the light of the minority policy of the Polish state: It pursued, albeit not always with the same intensity in the various phases, a policy of Polonization toward Ukrainians, which favored a turn toward the OUN, especially among the ranks of disaffected Western Ukrainian youth.

The OUN's terror in the 1930s included actions against Jews (for example, burning down Jewish stores), in which physical violence was also used. The OUN's anti-Semitism was still predominantly economically rather than racially motivated during this period. In their view, the Jewish population dominated urban commerce, blocking the formation of a Ukrainian middle class and, thus, the full nation-building of Ukrainians. The anti-Semitic stereotype of "the Jews as vicarious agents of the Russians" – or the Soviets – was already in place in Dontsov's work in the mid-1920s but had not yet come to the fore.

The OUN developed its most intensive political activity in Poland when Stepan Bandera became the leader of the OUN's national executive in the western Ukrainian territories. Born in 1909 in the eastern Galician village of Staryy Uhryniv (now Ivano-Frankivsk Oblast/Ukraine), Stepan Bandera grew up as the son of a Greek Catholic priest and came from the rural Ukrainian intelligentsia. He joined the OUN in 1929 and, by June 1932, had already risen to the position of deputy national leader and propaganda officer. As a country leader (unofficially as early as the end of 1932, officially since June 1933), Bandera bore responsibility for the OUN's assassinations, and under his leadership, the OUN's terror increased once again. Bandera advocated individual terror as part of a "permanent revolution" that would prepare Ukrainians for a "national revolution" to be sparked later. It would eventually lead to the establishment of a Ukrainian state. Under Bandera's responsibility as a national leader, the OUN carried out its most spectacular assassination: the murder of Polish Interior Minister Bronisław Pieracki in Warsaw on June 15, 1934.

Together with other members of the OUN, Bandera was tried in two trials in Warsaw and Lviv (formerly Lviv) in 1935 and 1936. He was sentenced to death, but the sentence was later commuted to life imprisonment. His appearance transformed even the first court trial in Warsaw, which attracted much media attention, into a propaganda success for the OUN. Bandera answered the judge's questions not in Polish but in Ukrainian, which was inadmissible. Because of this, he resisted and shouted accusations at the Polish state when he was led out of the courtroom. As a result of the court proceedings, Bandera became one of the best-known figures in western Ukraine. The indomitability and ideological perseverance demonstrated at the trials made him a "symbol of the upright Ukrainian nationalist who personified the slogan 'Win the Ukrainian state or die'." Both the 1935–36 trials and Bandera's assassination by a Soviet agent in Munich on October 15, 1959, are important starting points for glorifying this politician as the symbol of an indomitable victim nation. He was especially popular among the youth of western Ukraine.

The OUN was not able to establish a Ukrainian state on its own. Therefore, the question of with which alliance partner this goal could be achieved was of particular importance. As early as the 1920s, Dmytro Dontsov, with his figure of thought of "amorality," provided an argument that set the course early in the direction of Germany. In the spirit of his Russophobia, he demanded that the Ukrainian people could cooperate with any opponent of Russia without regard to their political goals. The OUN derived a corresponding preference from this early on, with common interests rather than ideological affinity being the deciding factor. After 1933, the National Socialist German Reich, which was fundamentally anti-Polish and anti-Soviet with a few tactical exceptions, came into question as an ally that could change the status quo in Europe. Because Poland, along with the Soviet Union, was initially the OUN's main enemy, the organization also maintained contacts with states whose relations with Poland were tense, such as Lithuania and Czechoslovakia.

Affinities between the ideology of the OUN and National Socialism, which later came to the fore, especially regarding anti-Bolshevism and anti-Semitism, facilitated cooperation. By the end of the 1930s, a racially argued anti-Semitism that excluded the assimilation of Jews had found its way into the OUN's ideological discourse, and by 1940/41, anti-Semitism in the form of the stereotype of "Jewish Bolshevism" (also "Judenkommune") formed an integral part of OUN ideology and policy.

As for the OUN's relationship with the Germans, this work will focus on a high point in the complex history of collaboration: the cooperation of the Bandera-led wing of the OUN with Nazi Germany in 1940/41.

After the assassination of its leader Yevhen Konovalets by the Soviet agent Sudoplatov in May 1938, conflicts arose within the OUN and in 1940, the organization split. One wing (OUN-M), led by Colonel Andrij Melnyk, tended to represent the older generation of the OUN, the émigrés; the other wing (OUN-B) was based in western Ukraine and German-occupied Poland and was led by Stepan Bandera. In terms of ideology, no significant differences existed. Both wings cooperated with the Germans. The OUN-M cooperated with the German police forces, among others, while the OUN-B cooperated primarily with the German Wehrmacht, especially its intelligence service, the *Abwehr*. The OUN-M, which acted more cautiously toward the Germans, was more willing to accept national setbacks on the road to statehood and initially limited itself to building pre-state-local structures. The emphatically activist Bandera-OUN relied more on its own initiative: Immediately after the liberation of the Ukrainian territories, it wanted to proclaim the state, form a government and begin building state structures — at the same time as the armed uprising of the Ukrainians. In Bandera's eyes, through such a "national revolution" led by the OUN-B, Ukrainians were to legitimize their claim to determine their destiny on Ukrainian territory to the Germans. These ideas are documented in *Struggle and Activity of the OUN during the War*, dated May 1941. The document, which Bandera wrote together with the cadres he appointed to the OUN-B leadership — including his deputy Yaroslav Stetsko (1912–1986) and the head of the OUN-B military staff and later commander-in-chief of the Ukrainian Insurgent Army (UPA) Roman Shukhevych (1907–1950) — contains detailed instructions for the expected German attack on the Soviet Union.

The instructions of the OUN-B defined the enemies from whom the liberated Ukrainian territory was to be "cleansed." In the event of war, the intelligentsia loyal to the regime, the activists and functionaries of the enemy nationalities, that is, the "Muscovites" as well as Poles and Jews, were to be liquidated and replaced by members of the Ukrainian elite. These instructions must always be seen in the light of the desired goal of an ethnically homogeneous territory and the OUN-B's high propensity for violence. As the main enemy, "Muscovite Bolshevism" came to the fore, with which the stereotype of Jews as pillars of Bolshevik rule ("Jewish commune") was linked. No distinction is made in the document between Jews as Soviet functionaries and other Jewish people; rather, a generalizing tendency to declare the Jewish people as a national collective enemy dominates. Ukrainians associated with the Soviet regime were also considered enemies.

Nazi Germany was the ally of the OUN-B, with whose help the Soviet Union was to be defeated. This alliance policy was not changed because, in the preceding years, the German side had always disappointed Ukrainian hopes for a state of their own—the primary goal of the OUN. Even the brutal anti-Jewish and anti-Polish terror of the Germans in Poland, of which the OUN was aware, did not diminish loyalty. On the contrary, the murderous program formulated in the instructions illustrates a clear radicalization and adaptation of the OUN to the policies of Nazi Germany. Representatives of the Wehrmacht, which cooperated with the OUN-B, may have been ambivalent about a certain degree of autonomy for the Ukrainians, but from Hitler's point of view, Ukraine did not have the role of an equal ally that the OUN-B desired. It was to become a colony; a Ukrainian state was not up for discussion.

Within the framework of military cooperation with the OUN-B, the Abwehr of the Wehrmacht deployed units with Ukrainian personnel. When the Battalion Nachtigall marched in, the OUN-B proclaimed a sovereign Ukrainian state in Lviv on June 30, 1941. Bandera himself was not present; according to Grzegorz Rossoliński-Liebe, he was detained by the Germans in the "Generalgouvernement" shortly before the proclamation. They forbade him to come to Lviv. Bandera's deputy, Yaroslav Stezko, became the head of the government. The foundation of the state failed. The German occupation forces decided shortly after the proclamation to imprison those involved. Bandera and Stezko were arrested on July 5 and 9, respectively, in 1941 and taken to Berlin on the condition that they did not leave the city. Both refused to retract the act of establishing the state, but they and the OUN-B, respectively, made offers to the German side to continue collaboration by mid-August. The *banderovtsy* tried in vain to convince the Germans to stick to the Ukrainian ally and the Ukrainian state, which, they assured, would join a European order led by Nazi Germany.

Despite the failure to establish the state, the OUN-B mobilized a considerable part of the West Ukrainian population with the proclamation of June 30, 1941, presenting its movement as the leading Ukrainian force and asserting its absolute claim to power in the Ukrainian camp. In state history books published since 1994, the "act of renewal of the Ukrainian state" is positively acknowledged as the "renewal of Ukrainian statehood," with few exceptions. The form of the Ukrainian state envisaged by the OUN-B, namely a totalitarian dictatorship under its leadership, is hardly mentioned in the state-fixated school history picture. The same applies to the fact that Bandera's state project stood primarily for integrating an autonomous Ukraine into Hitler's Europe and thus came far closer to the fascist satellite state of the Croatian Ustasha than to real independence.

Although the Germans disappointed Ukrainians' hopes for a separate state, the OUN-B initially continued cooperating with the German occupiers in July 1941. Among the darkest chapters of the OUN-B's history, and one that is largely taboo in today's debates on Ukrainian history is the participation of the OUN-B and the Ukrainian militias it led and raised in the pogroms against the Jewish population that began in numerous towns and villages in western Ukraine after the withdrawal of the Red Army—and almost simultaneously with the OUN-B's "act of state" — in late June/early July 1941. The same applies to the assistance provided by the militias — through arrests of Jews — in mass shootings in July 1941 by the Einsatzgruppen. The militias were also involved in mass killings by the Waffen SS Viking Division in a number of towns in eastern Galicia. The historian Aleksandr Kruglov estimates the number of Jews murdered throughout western Ukraine in June/July 1941 to be about 16,000.

The anti-Jewish violence was justified by the ideology that Jews were generally to be classified as supporters of the Soviet regime. The immediate trigger of the pogroms, of which only the case of Lviv can be briefly considered here (June 30–July 2, 1941), was, among other things, the discovery of the prison inmates murdered by the Soviets or by the Soviet secret police NKVD during the withdrawal of the Red Army (among whom were mostly Ukrainians, but also many Poles and Jews). Reasons for imprisonment by the NKVD included suspicion of Ukrainian nationalism or links to the nationalist underground. The total number of inmates (Ukrainians, Jews, and Poles) imprisoned by the NKVD and killed during the withdrawal of the Red Army was over 3,000 in Lviv alone; for all areas of Soviet-occupied eastern Poland, it is estimated at over 20,000, two-thirds of them in western Ukraine alone.

The rapid dissemination of information about the mass murders of prison inmates and the fact that Jews were used to clean up and recover bodies in the NKVD prisons acted as a catalyst for pogrom-like anti-Jewish violence. The Ukrainian militias forcibly took the Jews — in far greater numbers than needed for the cleanup work — to the prisons, abused and beat them, assisted by civilians and civilian women. Abuses and killings in the prison yards mostly involved Ukrainian militia, civilians, German soldiers and police. The Ukrainian militia or locals killed the Jewish population in the context of participating in violent excesses; the Ukrainian militia did not carry out systematic shootings. The German rulers tolerated and encouraged the outbreaks of hatred; the locals, however, did not have to be particularly driven to anti-Jewish acts. The violent excesses against Jews were, in the eyes of many Ukrainians, a punishment for Soviet crimes in the sense of the stereotypical perception of "Jewish Bolshevism" — also shared and spread by the OUN-B. According to Kai Struve, the acts of violence reflected the "emotional state of emergency" that the confrontation with the NKVD crimes triggered as much as the joy over the liberation from Soviet rule, of which the Jews were seen as the bearers and beneficiaries.

In addition, there was the euphoric hope of many Ukrainians for their own state, which was soon disappointed by the Germans. The militias led by the OUN-B were still assisting the German security police by making arrests in the mass shootings of Jews at the end of July/beginning of August. Although the OUN-B's relation-

ship with the Germans had soured massively after the failed founding of the state, its cooperation in acts of violence against Jews did
not contradict the OUN-B's goals. The latter saw the persecution of
Jews as a concrete field of cooperation and still hoped to convince
the Germans to allow the establishment of a Ukrainian state
through appropriate cooperation.

The violence of Ukrainian militias against Jews in many places
cannot be explained solely in terms of a struggle against Soviet
domination symbolized by Jews: In southeastern Galicia, in places
where the Hungarian occupation forces there did not exercise full
control (especially in the villages), the OUN-B-led militias killed
Polish and Ukrainian activists in their actions against real and perceived helpers of the Soviets, but entire families in the case of the
Jewish ones. This suggests that generalized and eliminatory anti-
Semitism also played a role in the actions of the Bandera militia as
an independent motive. Despite the significant involvement of
OUN-B members and other locals in the anti-Jewish violence, the
killing emanated from the Germans to a far greater degree. Moreover, Ukrainian militias did not act uniformly toward Jews in all lo-
cations. Despite the massive anti-Jewish violence perpetrated by
the Ukrainian side in the summer of 1941, the prejudice of "anti-
Semitism of Ukrainians" is as false as other collective stereotypes.
Thousands of Jews were helped or saved by Ukrainians during the
occupation.

In August and September 1941, the Germans finally termi-
nated cooperation with the Bandera OUN. The German occupation
forces now took selective action — though not on a broad front —
against the organization in the form of arrests and shootings. Bandera was sent to Sachsenhausen concentration camp in November
1941 in "Ehrenhaft" (honourably). His brothers, OUN-B members
Oleksandr and Vasyl, were arrested by the Gestapo in the fall of
1941 and murdered in the Auschwitz concentration camp in July
1942. In the summer of 1942, other members of the OUN-B leadership group were deported to Auschwitz.

Forced into illegality, the OUN-B had to rebuild itself. Under
its leadership, the Ukrainian Insurgent Army (UPA) was established in 1942/43, which was basically its military arm, though not

completely identical to the OUN-B. The personnel base of the UPA was recruited, among others, from members of the OUN-B, former members of the Nachtigall and Roland battalions belonging to the OUN-B, as well as local young men and parts of the Ukrainian "auxiliary police," many of whom had participated in the German mass murders of Jews and then deserted to the UPA. In the course of the war, the UPA gained increasing political importance. It had broad support among the western Ukrainian population, which still had memories of the repressive Soviet rule during 1939–1941 as fresh as they were bad and feared its return to western Ukraine in the summer of 1944. The UPA's struggle, concentrated in western Ukraine, lasted until 1949, while the anti-Soviet resistance of the nationalist underground lasted until the 1950s.

From the summer of 1943, the UPA fought mainly against Soviet partisans, whose emergence in Volhynia had been a motive of its foundation, and in 1944, after the recapture of the territories by the Soviets, it also fought against the Red Army. It also cracked down on Polish residents. The UPA's war with the Soviets was fought with enormous brutality on both sides. To deprive the UPA of its recruiting base and support, the Soviet secret police responded with mass shootings, arrests, and deportations. Between 1944 and 1952, about 153,000 people were shot, and between 1944 and 1953, about 66,000 families (about 204,000 people) were deported from western Ukraine. This is one reason for the anti-Soviet-tinged national memory culture that dominates eastern Galicia and parts of Volhynia, where the UPA is seen as a kind of homeland security army.

In Soviet historiography and propaganda, numerous aspects of the underground struggle of the UPA were concealed, and the stereotypes of the *banderovtsy* were transferred to the UPA. The resulting distorted image of the UPA's continuous collaboration with the Germans, which is mostly adopted by today's Russian media propaganda, is, however, historically inaccurate in this unambiguousness. Although there were individual contacts of UPA groups with German authorities, the nationalist partisan struggle of the UPA also tended to turn against the German occupying power. For example, the UPA's actions were directed against the German civil administration and infrastructure and were "not isolated cases, but noticeably restricted their work." In addition, the UPA attempted to free forced laborers, not least by incorporating them into the UPA. The UPA's resistance was directed primarily against the civil administration, the German security police and the SD, but hardly against the Wehrmacht.

In much of Ukrainian historiography, the UPA, steeped in Cossack traditions, is portrayed as a "national army" and a third force that fought uncompromisingly against the German and Soviet occupation forces.

In addition, it is pointed out that during the extraordinary congress of the OUN-B in August 1943, there were considerable modifications in the program of the OUN and UPA in the direction of democratization and the sense of a more moderate attitude of the UPA towards Jews. However, the resulting image of the UPA as an anti-totalitarian force fighting for the freedom and independence of Ukraine can only be maintained if the dark sides of the UPA are consistently suppressed. Democratization was only on paper and was motivated primarily by tactics: Faced with the imminent defeat of the German Reich, the OUN-B and the UPA sought new allies, such as the Western powers.

The UPA perpetuated many elements of the far-right integral nationalism of the OUN of the 1930s. The real crime of the UPA began in March 1943 with the attempt at ethnic cleansing of the Volhynia region. The terror against the Polish population was aimed at the ethnic homogenization of Volhynia to underline the claim of inclusion of this region in a future Ukrainian state. At least 60,000 Poles fell victim to the massacres, and allegedly 15,000–20,000 Ukrainians to the countermeasures of the Polish Home Army.[1] This event is part of a larger bloody Ukrainian-Polish conflict, also known under the name Volhynia tragedy, which is used mainly in Ukraine and has not been sufficiently researched or reappraised so far.

---

1   Kappeler, Andreas: "Kleine Geschichte der Ukraine," pp. 222-223, C. H. Beck, Munich 2014.

The UPA's treatment of the Jewish population, who fled into the woods or worked in UPA ranks as doctors or artisans, also still requires thorough investigation. However, the UPA's attitude tended to remain anti-Semitic. Many UPA partisans remained convinced that "the Jews" supported Soviet power. In the spring of 1944, cooperation between the UPA and the Wehrmacht resumed. According to recent research, at least 1,000 to 2,000 Jews who had fled into the forests were killed by UPA units in Volhynia alone.[2]

After western Ukraine was once again in Soviet hands, Stepan Bandera was released from prison in September 1944 — another consequence of the OUN's renewed cooperation with the Germans. He remained the symbolic leader of the OUN-B during the war but had little to do with the UPA's struggle. Bandera still took part in the last stage of the Ukrainian-German collaboration history: In November 1944, he was a co-founder of the Ukrainian National Committee, which the German Reich government still recognized in March 1945 as the "sole representative of the Ukrainian people," but in the future, neither he nor the OUN-B played a decisive role there. From February 1945, Bandera headed the organization's foreign center, which had been founded at a Vienna conference of the OUN-B, before moving to Bavaria after the end of the war, where he lived under a false name until his assassination in 1959. The OUN-B's foreign organization remained embroiled in ideological squabbles and power-political conflicts after the war and eventually split. Stepan Bandera is said to have resisted democratization tendencies in the organization's internal struggles, although it is unclear whether his rivals' democratic change efforts were serious. In any case, Bandera ultimately headed a wing of the OUN-B abroad, whose activities were largely limited to exile. On the one hand, the OUN-B leadership abroad and the country structures of the OUN and UPA in Ukraine increasingly isolated themselves from one another. A few years after the end of the war, the OUN abroad no longer had a base in the Ukrainian homeland.

---

2   Cf. research by Jared Graham McBride, Los Angeles. I would like to thank Dieter Pohl for the reference to this research.

In Russian TV propaganda, it was easy to find the symbols of the radical nationalist tradition visible on the Maidan, complete with portraits of Bandera, and put them front and center to support their falsifying theses about the "new *banderovtsy* visually." At the regular large "people's rallies," the centerpiece of the Maidan protests, an overwhelming majority used not the signs of the nationalist tradition but the state symbols of Ukraine, especially the blue-and-yellow flag and this often in combination with the EU flag. Acceptance of Bandera, popular primarily among western Ukrainian (eastern Galician) demonstrators, also grew during the protests among Kyiv and central Ukrainian demonstrators, who formed the majority at the large "people's assemblies." However, neither among these demonstrators nor among a majority of the population did he rise to become an undisputed national hero.

In the years following the Maidan, approval ratings for Stepan Bandera, always a controversial figure in Ukraine, have risen slightly in polls, but not massively. According to a representative poll conducted by the Ukrainian sociological group *Rejtynh* [Rating] in October 2018, slightly more than one-third of respondents expressed a positive attitude toward Bandera (18 percent "quite positive"; 18 percent "somewhat positive"), putting him in sixth place among ten possible historical figures, still behind former CPSU General Secretary Leonid Brezhnev. Bandera's ratings are nowhere near the top ratings of the traditionally popular Cossack heretic Bohdan Khmelnytsky (73 percent, first place) or the "father of Ukrainian historiography," Mykhailo Hrushevsky (68 percent, second place), who represents a moderate national view of history. Even in central Ukraine, he only received 35 percent, while the high positive ratings in western Ukraine (64 percent), where honoring the memory of the protagonists of the OUN and UPA has traditionally been a high priority, are just as unsurprising as the significantly lower approval ratings in the south and east of the country (17 percent each).

Even the commemorative days associated with him and the OUN-B, the red-and-black organizational flag of the OUN and his portrait failed to establish themselves as a representative symbol of the Maidan movement. The most important symbol was Taras

Shevchenko, the undisputed Ukrainian national *dichter* [poet] among almost all Ukrainians. His image, affixed to the large Euro-banner visible from afar, remained on the stage from the beginning to the end of the protests.

The only element of the radical nationalist tradition that gained wide currency was the cry "Glory to Ukraine, glory to the heroes!" as the OUN also used it as a greeting. Its popularization on the Maidan and afterward does not imply approval of a fascist program, nor is it primarily linked to the memory of the historical OUN or UPA. For most protesters, the cry "Glory to Ukraine" connects with the concrete heroes of the Maidan, such as the protesters killed in late February. It stands for democratic change and revolt against an authoritarian and corrupt regime.

The image of Stepan Bandera as an indomitable fighter for Ukrainian independence and against the totalitarian occupiers, which is particularly popular among young people, is nevertheless based on a misrepresentation of history. Historically, Bandera stands for the most extreme form of nationalism, where dissenters had no place. It is, therefore, questionable whether a radical nationalist tradition transfigured in terms of freedom will be suitable as a symbolic resource for a democratic society.

Particularly in the eastern Ukrainian Donbas, but also in parts of the south, which is now predominantly loyal to the state, the popularization of nationalist symbols is radically rejected or viewed with skepticism and can contribute to alienation from the Ukrainian state. This is certainly also, but not in every case, solely a consequence of Soviet and Russian propaganda. Political symbols cannot be easily separated from their historical meanings, or different family experiences passed down orally. Finally, people in the Donbas and parts of the south lacked the emancipation experience of the Maidan. It has, therefore, hardly been possible for them to comprehend the liberal-democratic reevaluations of individual nationalist symbols that the protests brought about or confirmed. This, in turn, has made it difficult for them to really trust the shift in meaning. Ukrainian society will therefore have to face an open and domination-free debate about the history of OUN and UPA in the future, which also does not conceal the dark sides.

Acknowledgments

The author would like to thank Frank Golczewski, Dieter Pohl, Ray Brandon, Kai Struve, and Grzegorz Rossoliński-Liebe for their important comments.

This article is a revised version of the original chapter: "Stepan Bandera — Zum historischen und politischen Hintergrund einer Symbolfigur," in: Katharina Raabe (ed.): *Gefährdete Nachbarschaften: Ukraine, Russland, Europäische Union*, 103-123, Wallstein, Göttingen 2015.

Literature

Bruder, Franziska: *"Den ukrainischen Staat erkämpfen oder sterben!" Die Organisation ukrainischer Nationalisten (OUN) 1929-1948*, Metropol, Berlin 2006.

Kappeler, Andreas: *Kleine Geschichte der Ukraine*, C.H. Beck, München 2014.

Petrenko, Olena: *Unter Männern: Frauen im ukrainischen nationalistischen Untergrund 1944-1954*, Ferdinand Schöningh, Paderborn 2018.

Struve, Kai: "Tremors in the Shatterzone of Empires: Eastern Galicia in Summer 1941," in: Omer Bartov and Eric D. Weitz (eds.): *Shatterzone of Empires: Coexistence and Violence in the German, Habsburg, Russian, and Ottoman Borderlands*, 463-484, Indiana University Press, Bloomington 2013.

Struve, Kai: *Deutsche Herrschaft, ukrainischer Nationalismus, antijüdische Gewalt Der Sommer 1941 in der Westukraine*, De Gryuter, Berlin 2015.

Struve, Kai: "Das Einsatzkommando Lemberg, die ukrainische Miliz und die 'Petljura-Tage' am 25. und 26. Juli 1941," https://www.academia.edu/3721431/Das_Einsatzkommando_Lemberg_die_ukrainische_Miliz_und_die_Petljura-Tage_am_25._und_26_Juli_1941

Veselova, Oleksandra M. and Kulčyc'kyj, Stanislav V. (eds.): *OUN v 1941 rotsi: Dokumenty*, Vol. 1, NANU, Kyiv 2006.

Rossoliński-Liebe, Grzegorz: *Stepan Bandera: The Life and Afterlife of a Ukrainian Nationalist*, ibidem-Verlag, Stuttgart 2014.

The Forgotten Koriukivka Massacre

Christoph Brumme

Koriukivka is a settlement in northeastern Ukraine, Chernihiv region. On the night of February 27, 1943, Soviet partisans attack a German-Hungarian garrison at the railroad station of Koriukivka. According to their own reports, they kill 78 soldiers and take some prisoners. They manage to free 97 prisoners, among them the sons of the commander of the partisans, Theodosius Stupak. He dies in action. In a report to Moscow, the partisans destroy, among other things, a telephone station, a mechanical workshop, a fuel depot with gasoline, eighteen railroad cars, and the building of the State Bank after blowing up a safe there and stealing 320,000 Soviet rubles.

As revenge for the attack, the SS and the Hungarian military police plan a "punitive action" against the inhabitants of Korjukiwka. As far as is known, the order is given by the chief of staff of the Wehrmacht command in the neighboring district of Konotop, Lieutenant Colonel Bruno Franz Bayer (in some sources, also spelled Baier or Beyer, in others, he appears only as Bruno Franz). SS Sonderkommando 4 a is in charge of the "punitive action." The SS men had already committed numerous war crimes and mass murders, including the massacres of the Jewish people from Kyiv in Babyn Yar, with more than 33,000 victims and Poltava, with several thousand victims. In March 1943, in Sumy, they shot 250 Hungarian Jews who belonged to a labor company of the Hungarian army.

On the morning of March 1, 1943, the SS and Hungarian units, probably supported by local Soviet "auxiliary" police, surround the settlement of Koriukivka. The death squads search the town's buildings, set fire to houses, herd people into large buildings like the theater or a restaurant and shoot them there or throw them alive into the fire. About 500 people are killed in the restaurant, and only five survive. A total of 6700 people is murdered on March 1 and 2.

1290 houses are burned down, and only ten brick buildings remain. Witnesses will later testify that smoke and fire from the fires could still be seen more than twenty kilometers away in surrounding settlements. On March 9, the murder squads return to kill the survivors. Only 1893 victims can be identified, including 704 children and teenagers and 1097 women. Most of them, 1715 people, are of Ukrainian nationality.

Worse than Lidice and Oradour – but the massacre fits into the concept of Soviet propaganda

The Koriukivka massacre was the largest punitive action in World War II against the non-Jewish population, not only on the territory of the Soviet Union but in the whole of Europe. While the SS massacres in the Czech village of Lidice, with 173 murdered or in the French Oradour, with 642 victims, have become internationally known and have been depicted in quite a few books and films, the terrible crime in Koriukivka with so many more victims is unknown even to many Ukrainians until today. Heinrich Mann published a novel of the same name about the Lidice bloodbath the following year. The tragedy of Koriukivka has been published until today only in some brochures and a single book with an edition of 500 copies, the historical-scientific study *Everyone has his own truth. Truth one: Koriukivka: a lifelong pain* by Vasily Ustimenko. Ustimenko financed it with his pension, as he said in his speech in 2013 during the book presentation. He had not found a sponsor. In his study, he tries to answer why the tragedy took place and whether it would have been possible to prevent it.

At least the Soviet partisans could probably have hindered the murder orgies of the Germans and the Hungarians very much, for there were only 300 to 500 perpetrators who carried out this war crime against the civilian population, while the partisans had over 5500 fighters in the surrounding villages and forests.

"There was no order from headquarters. So, we just sat and watched," summed up a Soviet partisan after the war. The top commander of the partisans, Oleksiy Fedorov, a two-time hero of the Soviet Union, was not present during the Koriukivka massacre but picked up new directives from Moscow. In his memoirs, he briefly refers to the events: "The comrades informed us about the main military operations that were carried out in our absence. The most interesting and successful was the raid on the Koriukivka garrison. Our boys have not forgotten this small town."[1] Fedorov does not mention a single word about the terrible murder of almost 7000 villagers—as if they did not exist!

The atrocious crimes of the National Socialists certainly fit into the concept of Soviet propaganda, as macabre as that sounds today. The orders of the Soviet military headquarters to partisan movements in Ukraine were exclusively about sabotage and destruction of enemy forces. However, Ukrainian historians believe no official documents exist that instructed the Soviet partisans to protect the civilian population.

Ukrainian historian Serhiy Butko, a member of the Ukrainian Institute of National Memory in Chernihiv oblast, explains it as follows:

> No punitive operations instigated by the Nazis against the local population were interrupted by the Soviet partisans, as this perfectly served the Bolshevik cause, the Germans committed so many atrocities as possible. The Bolshevik policy was to prove to the civilian population that the atrocities committed by the Nazi regime could not be compared to the Holodomor of 1932-33 and the Stalinist executions and repressions of the 1930s. Yes, the barbaric actions of the Nazis were indescribably horrible, but no better or worse than those committed by the Bolshevik regime[2].

Late commemoration

Only in 1977 in Koriukivka a granite monument was erected with the official name "In honor of the heroic resistance of the population against German fascist invaders." The creator of the monument is the famous Ukrainian sculptor Inna Kolomyez.

---

1   "Bloody March 1943: What is known about the Koryukov tragedy and why is it important to know about it?", 03/01/2018, https://112.ua/obshchestvo/kr ovavyy-mart-1943-goda-chto-izvestno-o-koryukovskoytragedii-i-pochemu-o-ney-vazhno-znat-435079.html

2   Euromaidan Press, Christine Chraibi: The forgotten tragedy of Koryukovka: How the Nazis exterminated a town of 7,000 souls.

However, the massacre did not make it into the Soviet canon of heroic stories and heinous crimes. Serhiy Butko cites the reason: "Of course, one wonders where the partisans were when the population of Koriukivka was massacred." At least in this gruesome case, they had just not been the "avengers of the people."

It was not until the seventieth anniversary of the tragedy on March 2, 2013, that the Ukrainian state adopted special measures to commemorate the victims of this war crime by decree of President Viktor Yanukovych. On the anniversary in 2018, many television programs commemorated the terrible events with permanently switched-on memorial candles.

However, a high-ranking Ukrainian politician has never visited the memorial ceremonies in Koriukivka. Thus, one should not be surprised that, apparently, only one German politician has made his way to Koriukivka. In March 2005, the German ambassador Dietmar Stüdemann commemorated the murdered people there. The ambassador said in front of hundreds of people at the mourning rally:

> We Germans know exactly what the Nazis did in your country. After the death of Koriukivka, Nazi Germany also died. Years passed. Both Germany and Koriukivka revived. Ukraine became independent. The peoples of both countries shake hands over the graves of the dead, although our guilt is great. But human friendship can do much, very much, and this gives hope that war will not happen again, fascism will not be revived.[3]

The people of Koriukivka have long tried to find a twin town in Germany, according to *taz* [*die Tageszeitung*] reporter Bernhard Clasen in May 2015. He is apparently the only German journalist so far to have visited the crime scene and reported on it ("Uncle, don't shoot, I want to live!"). However, a partnership between Koriukivka and a German city has still not been established.

---

3   Ibid.

Babyn Jar

Bremen Police Officers in the Holocaust

Klaus Wolschner

The fact that, in addition to the men of the SS, soldiers of the Wehrmacht and thousands of German police officers in Eastern Europe were involved in the mass murders of Jews could not be a secret in postwar German society – there were too many people in the know. However, the perpetrators did not speak about it voluntarily in public. It took decades for historians to come to terms with the subject.[1] A former police officer and historian, Karl Schneider has reconstructed the history of the Bremen Police Battalions, primarily from the files of investigations by the public prosecutor's office. His commendable 800-page work, published in 2011 under the title: *Auswärts eingesetzt' – Bremer Polizeibataillone und der Holocaust*, should be referred to here.

Babyn Yar is the name of a ravine, where in 1941, more than 33,000 Jewish People from Kyiv were murdered. Several hundred policemen of the Bremen Police Battalion 303 were among them. They drove Jews to the firing squads and were possibly even involved in the murders themselves. For the police officers involved, Babyn Yar was still regarded 25 years later as the date of a turning point – after Babyn Yar, the killing really began.

No one was prosecuted after the war. In the 1950s, the Bremen Senate not only reinstated around 70 men from the Bremen Police Battalions in the police service, but it also actively pursued the early release from prison of Erwin Schulz, the former Bremen Gestapo chief who had been convicted as a war criminal. Karl Schulz, who, according to Schneider, was "involved in National Socialist crimes," was even able to become Bremen's criminal director in 1952. The Bremen Public Prosecutor's office did not investigate the

---

1   It was not until 1992 that the work of the American Christopher Browning on the "ordinary men" appeared (Engl: "Ordinary men: Reserve Police Battalion 101 and the final solution in Poland"). In 2005, Stefan Klemp published his handbook on the failure of post-war justice: "Nicht ermittelt. Police Battalions and Postwar Justice.

members of Bremen's Police Battalion 105 until the 1960s, and it discontinued the proceedings in 1968. A search in the Bremen "Weser-Kurier" archives under the keyword "police battalion" does not yield a single report on the crimes of the police battalions until 2007. It was not until half a century later that Bremen's senator of the interior informed the public about the role of the police in the Nazi era and the police battalion in an exhibition.

Bremen 1935: Police units are incorporated into the Wehrmacht.
Photo: Hermann Reil

Police operations abroad before 1941

Shortly after seizing power in 1933, the National Socialist regime began to expand the police force and deploy it abroad. Thus, police officers volunteered for service in Southwest Africa (today: Namibia). At dawn on March 11, 1938, a long convoy of Bremen police officers set off south with an unknown destination—no one was supposed to know that the Anschluss of Austria was planned for May 13, 1938. The Bremen police officers had security duties in Linz, Krems and Wiener Neustadt and had to march mainly to demonstrate power. They were greeted with cheers and flowers, and they reported back home. Moreover, Jews who were picked up were forced to wash the Bremen police cars. The Bremen police were also present at the Anschluss [union] of the Sudentenland.

One participant noted in his diary that he was given cookies, cigarettes and chocolate.

Deployment in Ukraine

After missions in Norway and the Baltic States, the operation against the Soviet Union began in June 1941. Under the leadership of Heinrich Hannibal, who was never convicted for his crimes, the Bremen Police Battalion 303 advanced to the oil center of Boryslaw and then to Lviv. There, German troops had found about 4000 corpses in Lonzky Prison—apparently political prisoners murdered by Soviet intelligence. The Lviv population blamed "the Jews" for the crimes of the Stalinist regime—a hunt began among the local Lviv population in the power vacuum when the Germans approached. "In any case, we were strictly forbidden to interfere," reported one of the German police officers. After a few days, Commander Hannibal moved on with his Police Battalion 303.

Police Battalion 303 was already directly involved in the murder of the Jewish population "before Babyn Yar". The Regensburg public prosecutor's office took the number of murdered Jews from the so-called success reports of the Southern Police Regiment—more than 10,000 people were killed alone between August 25, 1941, and September 21, 1941. The Regensburg prosecutor's office assumed Bremen's Battalion 303 was directly involved in the killings as it moved from Lviv toward Kyiv. "There will have been few comrades from the company who did not take part in the shootings, unless they were on leave [...]" one of those involved in the investigation explained.

At the end of September, Einsatzkommando 5 was transferred to Kyiv, as was Police Battalion 303. In retaliation for bombings by the Ukrainian resistance after the capture of Kyiv on September 19, 1941, the SS had decided to exterminate the Jewish population of Kyiv. A ravine near the city was chosen as the murder site: Babyn Jar, in German "Weiberschlucht"—200 meters wide and 53 meters deep. The area was cordoned off by Police Battalion 45 and the Bremen Police Battalion 303 under its commander Major Heinrich Hannibal.

On September 28, 1941, they posted 2,000 posters in the city saying where Jewish people should gather on the morning of September 29. "To bring with them: Papers, money, valuables, and warm clothing. Those who do not comply will be shot," the posters said. At the same time, the rumor was spread that the city's Jewish population would be relocated. "Although at first only 5,000 to 6,000 Jews were expected to participate, more than 30,000 Jewish people turned up who, as a result of an exceedingly skillful organization, still believed in their resettlement until immediately before the execution." Some had even assumed that they would be resettled in Palestine.

To prevent escape attempts, the entire area was widely secured with barbed wire and order police. When the Jews approached the ravine, they were forced to hand over their jewelry, suitcases and fur coats and to undress. In groups of ten, they were ordered to step to the edge of the ravine. There they were shot down. An airplane flew over the ravine to drown out the shouting, and music sounded. Several groups of Sonderkommando 4 a were firing, with each unit taking turns after a few hours. The earth continued to move in some places for days because not all the Jewish people were dead when the earth buried them. The massacre lasted for two days. For days the murderers counted the money they had taken from the Jewish victims—millions must have been sent to Berlin packed in sacks.

All battalions deployed in Kyiv received an additional liquor ration, and some police officers sent gold coins and precious stones to their loved ones in Bremen.

Babyn Yar: The perpetrators later described details of the execution in interrogations

Driver Fritz Höfer, Einsatzkommando 4 a (interrogation 1959):

"The unclothed Jews were led into a ravine [...] When they arrived at the edge of the ravine, they were seized by officers of the Schutzpolizei and placed on top of Jews who had already been shot. This all happened very quickly. The corpses were literally piled up. Just as a Jew lay there, a gunman from the Schutzpolizei with the machine gun and shot the one lying there by shooting him in the neck. The Jews who came to the ravine were so shocked by the sight of this gruesome image that they were completely willless."

Kurt Werner, Sonderkommando 4 a (interrogation 1964):

"Immediately after my arrival at the execution site, I had to go down into this trough together with other comrades. The Jews had to lie down against the walls of the trough with their faces to the ground. In the trough there were three groups with marksmen, with a total of about twelve marksmen. At the same time, Jews were fed to these firing squads from above. The following Jews had to lie down on the corpses of the previously shot Jews. The shooters stood behind the Jews and killed them with shots to the neck. I still remember the horror of the Jews who, at the top of the pit, could look down on the corpses in the pit for the first time."

Whether the police battalion 303 in Babyn Yar "only" aided and abetted the mass murder or whether individual members were involved in the shooting is unclear from the documents. From this point of view, the statements of the Bremen police officer Ulrich Panzer are interesting. His father, Rudolf Panzer, was an instructor of the police battalion 303 in the police school in Bremen-Borgfeld. Some police officers from Police Battalion 303 had sought contact with his father after the war, his son recalls. At the meetings of the old comrades, the door was locked, and the son got only one or other remark. "They didn't just do the barricading; they were there for the shootings," he is convinced.

Processes discontinued

The Babyn Yar massacre was one of the charges in the Nuremberg trials. None of the Wehrmacht officers who participated in the preparation, execution or cover-up of the massacre had to stand trial.

The other police battalion formed in Bremen, number 105, helped in particular with the deportation of Dutch Jews to Auschwitz. For an assignment to Holland, there were additional days off, which is why service in the battalion was popular among Bremen police officers. The files of the Public Prosecutor's office from 1965 list a total of 48 cases in which the police battalion was involved in the murder of Dutch and Russian Jews. In 1968, the Bremen Public Prosecutor's office, headed by Siegfried Höffler, who had made a career as a public prosecutor during the Nazi era up to the People's Court, discontinued all proceedings with reference to S.47 of the Military Criminal Code — reason: no transgression of orders given, no discretionary powers.

Thus, the history of the Bremen Police Battalions confirms that they were "completely normal men" who had participated in the murder of the Jews while wearing police uniforms. They remained silent about their guilt after 1945, and they could remain silent because West German society largely avoided critical questions due to its entanglement with the Nazi regime. In Bremen, too, some of the alleged war criminals were "needed" to build the new state. This history was not dealt with until after a generational change.

Sources:

Schneider, Karl: *Auswärts eingesetzt – Bremer Polizeibataillone und der Holocaust*, Klartext Verlag, Essen 2011.

Wolschner, Klaus: "Polizisten als Täter: Die Helfer des Massakers von Babij Jar", in the *taz* of 08. 10. 2010.

The Antonescu Regime and the "Jewish Question" in Romania

Ottmar Traşcă

The anti-Semitic policies of the Antonescu regime during World War II have been studied by an increasing number of Romanian and international historians during the last decades. Especially after December 1989, a considerable number of contributions, studies and source editions were published. They deal with the position and role of the Jewish minority in Romanian society, its relations with the Romanian state, the anti-Semitic laws of the Antonescu regime and the deportation and extermination actions against the Jewish population from Bessarabia, Northern Bukovina and Transnistria.

According to the current state of research, it is clear from the investigations that the "Jewish Question" did not have a decisive influence on relations between Romania and the German Reich, at least for the period between September 1940 and December 1941. Even if the German Propaganda Minister Joseph Goebbels said in the fall of 1940: "The Jewish question is the core problem of Romania. Every 10th person a Jew," the "settlement of the Jewish question in Romania" was not a topic on the agenda of the high-level Romanian-German meetings, as had been the case with Hungary or Bulgaria. Between September 1940 and the end of 1941, the Third Reich did not pay special attention to implementing anti-Jewish measures in the allied states, such as Romania, nor did it put them under pressure.

In the one year between the defeat of France (June 1940) and the start of Operation Barbarossa (June 1941), the Madagascar Plan was on the agenda. The Foreign Office drew it up in cooperation with the Reich Security Main Office. It provided for the deportation of all Jews from Europe controlled by the Reich to the island of Madagascar. The plan became unfeasible after the Luftwaffe experienced defeat in the Battle of Britain, changing the military situation in Western Europe. Consequently, after the beginning of the German-Soviet War on June 22, 1941, a radical turn occurred in the policy propagated by the Third Reich in "Jewish affairs." However, the "Final Solution" — the physical extermination of the Jewish people — decided upon at the Wannsee Conference had long since begun in the East. In Romania, the implementation of anti-Semitic measures was realized on the initiative of the Antonescu regime. In this area, the Antonescu regime was "inspired" by the rich German "experience" in 1941/42.

With the establishment of the "national legionary" government in September 1940, a new wave of national "homogenization" policies began, the main goal of which was initially the removal of Jews from economic structures and managerial positions. Although "Romanianization" represented a goal that the Romanian political class had consistently pursued since the end of the 19th century, the "national legionary" regime differed radically from previous governments. This was because the so-called Romanianization process was directed almost exclusively against the Jewish minority. In doing so, the legionary movement resorted to terrorist methods that had not existed before in Romania's history.

Ion Antonescu's statements in January 1941 left no doubt about his intention to continue the anti-Semitic policy of the "national legionary" regime and to apply Nazi models in the "solution" of the "Jewish question."

The state leader already insulted the Jews as "enemies of the nation" or "mistletoes" when there was no pressure from the Third Reich. This rhetoric reflected his own convictions and already outlined the idea of the extermination of the Jews, which was then carried out by the Antonescu regime immediately after the outbreak of hostilities against the Soviet Union.

Concrete measures soon followed these statements. At the express request of the Romanian government, a group of 'German experts' arrived in the Romanian capital in March 1941 to 'advice' the Antonescu government. Among the Germans was SS-Sturmbannführer Gustav Richter, who, between April 1, 1941, and August 23, 1944, held the post of "advisor on Jewish and Aryanization issues" within the German legation in Bucharest. He was involved in the drafting of the new anti-Semitic laws based on the existing model in Germany, as well as in the preparation of the final "solution of the Jewish question" in Romania.

Massacre of Jews

Immediately after the beginning of the war against the Soviet Union, the Antonescu regime carried out massacres of Jews, carried out by the Romanian services (army, gendarmerie and police) in Jassy (today Iași), Bessarabia, Bukovina, Odesa and Transnistria. In the fall of 1941, survivors of this killing campaign were deported to camps and ghettos in Transnistria. The radicalism that characterized the implementation of the "Romanian solution to the Jewish question" — as it was called in the historiography — surprised even the leadership of the Third Reich. Thus, on August 19, 1941, Adolf Hitler told Propaganda Minister Joseph Goebbels: "And as far as the Jewish question is concerned, today, at any rate, we can state that, for example, a man like Antonescu is proceeding in this matter even more radically than we have done so far."

The Romanian Army joined the Wehrmacht in Operation Barbarossa. The joint Romanian-German military operations on the southern flank of the eastern Front, involving the 11th German Army and the 3rd and 4th Romanian Armies, led to the return of Bessarabia and Northern Bukovina to Romanian territory by the end of July 1941. These were the two Romanian provinces that the USSR had annexed as a result of two Soviet ultimatums in June 1940. According to the German-Romanian agreement of August 30, 1941, Transnistria, the area between the Dniester and the Bug rivers, was to be placed under the Romanian administration. Transnistria became, in a short time, a "real ethnic grave of Romania." Here, many Jews deported from other provinces of Romania and Ukraine met a miserable death. In the camps and ghettos of Transnistria alone, some 150,000 to 210,000 Jews perished between 1941 and 1944. For example, in the village of Bershad in the present-day Vinnytsia Oblast, the largest ghetto in Transnistria was established with 20,000 deported Jews from Bessarabia. In this ghetto, as in numerous other camps and colonies in Transnistria, a deadly typhus epidemic broke out in the winter of 1941/42. Approximately half of the 24,000 Jews living in Bershad before the epidemic outbreak died due to the typhus epidemic.

While the Romanian authorities took over the administration of the province of Transnistria, Marshal Ion Antonescu, after exchanging letters with Adolf Hitler, decided that the Romanian Army should continue military operations alongside the Wehrmacht and penetrate deeper into Soviet territory. In August 1941, units of the 3rd Romanian Army participated with the 11th German Army in the breakthrough of the "Stalin Defense Line" and subsequently in the great battle for Kyiv. The 4th Romanian Army had been ordered to capture Transnistria with its main port, Odesa.

The long siege of Odesa by the 4th Romanian Army (August 18–October 16, 1941) showed the Romanian Army's great deficiencies in training, equipment and command methods. As a result of the duration of the siege and the large losses suffered by the 4th Army, Marshal Antonescu's anti-Semitic rhetoric became radicalized. The scale of Romanian losses on the battlefield, as well as the fierce, almost fanatical resistance of the Soviet troops, led Marshal Antonescu to attribute more and more of the responsibility for this to the Jews from the conquered territories and the "Jewish-Bolshevik commissars."

This radicalization emerges, for example, from an instruction sent by Marshal Antonescu to Deputy Prime Minister Mihai Antonescu on September 5, 1941, to the front line outside Odesa.

> The front-line soldiers are in great danger of being wounded or killed because of the Jewish commissars who, with a diabolical tenacity, drive the Russians forward from behind with the revolver until they die to the last man in the positions. This I have learned and I am outraged.
>
> All Jews are to be returned to the camps, to be desired would be to those from Bessarabia, because I will deport them from there to Transnistria and would be immediately freed from my present worries. It is a fight to the death. It must be understandable for all that it is not a fight with the Slavs, but one with the Jews. Either we win and the world is purified, or they win and we become their slaves. Consequently, sparing them internally would be a weakness that would put our victory in jeopardy. In order to win, we must be resolute in our attitude. Everyone must know this. It is not the economy that takes precedence in these moments, but the will of the nation itself.

> The war in general and the battles of Odesa have proved with excess that Satan is the Jew. Hence our huge losses. Without the Jewish commissars, we would have been in Odesa long ago.

The linguistic aggressiveness of the directive and the insults Marshal Antonescu uses towards the Jews, as well as the absurd accusations the Romanian leader makes towards them, prove the purely racist character of Ion Antonescu's anti-Semitic views. Because of their radicalism and racist content, these statements can be equated with the anti-Semitism advocated by Adolf Hitler. This directive had decisive consequences for the Jews from Odesa and explained the harshness of the measures taken against them by the Romanian authorities.

The mass murder of the Jews of Odesa

In October 1941, there were 80,000 to 90,000 Jews living in Odesa who, quite contrary to official Romanian propaganda, had not been among the privileged of the Bolshevik regime. There is much evidence that the Soviet authorities executed hundreds of Jews under trumped-up pretexts during the siege of Odesa by the 4th Romanian Army. The Romanian military captured Odesa on October 16. During the long continuing siege of the city, elements of the 11th Army of the German Wehrmacht reinforced the Romanian troops. It was not a triumphal entry of a victorious army but rather the occupation of a city abandoned by its exhausted defenders, whose population despised the conquerors, regarding them as "starved and contemptible foreigners."

As expected, the expulsion and murder of the Jews from Odesa became the main goal of the new rulers from the first moment of the Romanian occupation. The fate of the Jews from Odesa was sealed by an attack on the afternoon of October 22, 1941, when the building of the Romanian city commander — the former NKVD building — was blown up. The reaction of the Romanian leader Antonescu was not long in coming. During October 22-23, 1941, Marshal Antonescu ordered the Romanian military services to carry out "drastic reprisals" against the Jewish population in Odesa. These orders resulted in a mass murder on October 24, 1941.

At least 22,000 Jews (according to other sources, there were 40,000) were herded by the Romanian military to Dalnik near Odesa and locked up in abandoned Red Army ammunition barracks. The warehouses were first machine-gunned and then set on fire. Mines were attached to one warehouse, and it was blown up at the same time the military command building had exploded, i.e., at 5:45 pm.

The Jews who survived these events in Odesa were deported at the beginning of 1942. The Romanian rule from October 17, 1941, to the middle of March 1942 — the deportation was mostly finished — became, for the Jews from Odesa, a synonym for a regime of terror and extermination. 25,000 to 40,000 Jewish people had been murdered, and about 60,000 Jews were deported.

The anti-Semitic policy of the Antonescu regime affected not only the Jews from Bukovina, Bessarabia and Transnistria but also the Jews from the Old Kingdom, which had already belonged to Romania before World War I, from Transylvania and Banat. Although the Jews from these provinces were treated better than their co-religionists from Bessarabia, Bukovina and Transnistria in 1941 and the first half of 1942, their fate hung by a hair in the summer of 1942. Ion Antonescu initially postponed their deportation, and at the end of 1942, he renounced the deportation. This development was influenced by the marshal's assessment that Germany had already lost the war after the defeat at Stalingrad. He wanted to resume contact with the allies with a view to getting out of the war. For the resumption of more or less official contact with the allies, a more "humane policy" toward the Jewish population in Romania could prove to be a precious political asset.

Moreover, the Antonescu government's agreement to let numerous Jews emigrate from Romania to Palestine in 1943 and 1944 had political and economic reasons. The regime received huge sums of money for the state account by introducing "emigration fees." Nazi Germany was visibly unhappy with the changes that began towards the end of 1942 in the anti-Semitic policies of the Romanian government. Nevertheless, Berlin repeatedly intervened unsuccessfully with the rulers in Bucharest.

Based on published and unpublished sources, it can be stated that the Antonescu regime's policy toward the Jews during World War II was determined by tactical and pragmatic considerations and generally followed Romania's foreign policy. Although the influence of Nazi Germany on the anti-Semitic policy of the cabinet under Marshal Ion Antonescu was felt, especially in 1941 and 1942, Germany could not impose the application of mass deportations on the Romanian government, as it happened, for example, in Croatia and Slovakia and — after March 19, 1944 — in Hungary. The establishment of ghettos, the deportations and massacres of hundreds of thousands of Jews in Bukovina, Bessarabia, Transnistria, Odesa, Iaşi and other places in 1941 and 1942, as well as the plans to deport the Jews from Banat, Southern Transylvania and the entire Romanian Old Kingdom, were mainly initiatives of the regime led by Marshal Ion Antonescu. Thus, the political and historical responsibility for these state crimes lies with Romania's head of state and the subordinate Romanian authorities.

Volodymyr Kolchinsky
A Life Story

Nikolaus von Twickel

Volodymyr Kolchinsky was one of the last survivors of the Odesa massacre. On May 16, 2020, he died in his hometown at 94.

In October 1941, a streetcar saved Volodymyr Kolchinsky's life. The then 16-year-old escaped the Odesa massacre, where some 25,000 people of predominantly Jewish origin were cruelly murdered by jumping into a parked streetcar.

On October 22, the German and Romanian occupiers in the port city on the Black Sea rounded up thousands of people in the city center and marched them through the city for hours. Among the victims were Kolchinsky, who came from a Jewish family, and his mother. His father, Yakov and his older brother fought in the ranks of the Red Army.

It was a death march. On the morning of October 22, a bomb in the Romanian headquarters killed many people, including the city commander Ion Glogojanu. The occupiers blamed Communists and Jews for the explosion and ordered mass arrests and executions. Jewish people were forced to gather at a factory in the center of the city.

Kolchinsky remembers that the central Preobrazhenska Street was lined with gallows with hanged people. The inscription "Partisan" was emblazoned on the dead bodies. Romanian soldiers with dogs herded the masses through the streets, older people, women and children; those who fell down were quickly dragged up again. The target was an abandoned ammunition depot along Ljustdorf Street, named after a seaside resort, founded by Black Sea Germans in the south of the city. Kolchinsky still has the images of that horrific day in his mind. He says the sound of the crowd was even more imprinted on his mind—"it was a booming babble of voices, " he says.

In the midst of this desperate situation, he managed to make a life-saving escape. Again and again, the 94-year-old recalls his mother's last words. She, who had otherwise always been gentle, stopped him and said sternly:

> We are led to die — but you, Volodya, must stay alive. And then dad will return and you have to tell him everything

In retrospect, that proved prophetic. "But how she knew that I can't tell you," he murmurs. Even today, Kolchinsky's memory brings tears to his eyes. "When I talk about it, I relive it all," he says. "I just had to do something," he continues. The decisive opportunity arose in a narrow street: "There was a (parked) streetcar, and the Romanians were forced to walk on the other side." Briefly out of sight of the overseers, he jumped into the carriage and hid under a bench seat. "I stayed there until it got dark." The other victims were locked in the ammunition barracks, which were then set on fire. Most of them burned alive. Those who tried to escape were killed by machine-gun salvos and hand grenades. Afterward, Kolchinsky recalls, "the smell of burnt flesh was in the air all over town."

When Soviet authorities dug for bodies at the site in 1944, the remains of more than 22,000 people were found. They were never buried.

The 16-year-old had remained alive, but for him, perhaps the most difficult time of his life began. Where was he to find shelter? Anyone who hid Jewish people risked being summarily shot. "I had nothing to eat, nothing to live in." A friend of Bulgarian descent took him in for a night but put him out in the morning because his parents did not want to take any risks. He was rescued by two teenage sisters who moved with him into an empty apartment and got him papers from a relative of the same age with which Kolchinsky could identify himself.

When Odesa was liberated in 1944, his father returned from a military hospital in Siberia — just as his mother had predicted. Kolchinsky, now of age, began non-commissioned officer training in the Red Army. For seven years, he served as a soldier. After leaving in 1951, he says, he had to start his life all over again. For 23 years, he worked in the Odesa Dzerzhinki Steelworks drawing workshop.

However, before that, Kolchinsky took part in the last battles of the Second World War. With a Soviet assault battalion, he advanced south across the Vistula River near Warsaw to the Oder River near Breslau, then advanced to Auschwitz. "It would be an understatement to say that we advanced. We rushed forward, fighting everything down," he recalled.

On January 27, 1945, Soviet troops liberated Auschwitz. What Kolchinsky remembers of the notorious concentration camp, apart from the huge gas ovens for burning corpses, is a storeroom where shoes, human hair and sacks of human ashes were neatly stored. Kolchinsky admits that it took him some time to understand the crime's dimension: "At first we didn't believe that such a thing would be done to exterminate Jews. It just seemed inhuman to us." However, Kolchinsky never developed hatred against Germany because of that. Years later, when he traveled to the GDR as a Soviet trade union official, his delegation was greeted by four-year-olds on their knees at a daycare center as "liberators." This was too much for him: "I took the kindergarten teacher aside and told her that this was exaggerated. You can't hold these children responsible for the mistakes of their fathers and grandfathers," he recalls.

The Center for Liberal Modernism is working to transform the Ljustdorf Street extermination site from a parking lot to a dignified memorial.

 This QR code will lead you to the video recording of our interview with Volodymyr Kolchinsky.

Chapter 3

Remembrance and Responsibility

Repressed Memories of the Holocaust

Irina Sherbakova

There were over three million Jews in the territories of the Soviet Union occupied by Hitler's army and its allies. According to different data, 2.6 to 2.8 million of them were murdered – almost half of all Jewish victims in Europe.

The extermination of Jews began in the first weeks after the beginning of the war in 1941 – through mass shootings, which in fact, happened in front of the eyes of the local populations. No one could claim they did not know what was happening to their Jewish neighbors.

The first reports of the mass murders of Jews reached the Soviet leadership very soon. In August 1941, a radio broadcast was organized in Moscow with well-known Jewish personalities calling on their fellow Jews to resist. In November 1941, the newspaper *Pravda* wrote about the mass murder of Jews in Kyiv – in Babyn Yar.

However, as early as 1942, Soviet propaganda, which constantly reported on the atrocities committed by the German occupiers, began to conceal the most terrible crime – the mass murders of the Jewish people. This was done to counteract the German propaganda, which proclaimed liberation from "Judeo-Bolshevism" and distributed leaflets with caricatures of Stalin depicting the Soviet leader with Semitic stereotypes and the Star of David.

The dormant anti-Semitism that never disappeared in the Soviet Union (despite its proclaimed internationalism) increased sharply in all occupied territories. The German invasion triggered pogroms against Jews in many places, especially in the territories annexed by the Soviet Union only after 1939. Some representatives of the local population entered service with the occupiers and took an active part in the extermination of the Jews. Nevertheless, even the rest of the population helped the Jews (looking for a hiding place or simply asking for bread and water) only in rare cases. The partisan groups refused to take in Jews who had fled into the forests, did not provide them with assistance, and were not asked to do so by the Soviet leadership.

The Stalinist leadership, which did not inform the general public about the mass murder of Jews, wanted to prevent the impression that the German occupiers saw only Jews and Communists as their enemies and that everyone else could continue to lead a "normal" life. Therefore, the Jews were not to be portrayed as the main victims. Thus, a veiling formula was created – one officially reported only victims among "peaceful Soviet citizens". Even when the Soviet press reported on the liberation of Auschwitz, it was not mentioned that mainly Jews had been murdered there.

This concealment was accompanied by a covert but clearly anti-Semitic course of the Soviet leadership. Beginning in the winter of 1942, the Department of Agitation and Propaganda of the Central Committee (CC) of the Communist Party issued instructions against "the nesting of the Jews" in various structures, especially in the ideological and cultural spheres. This led to the dismissal of Jews, primarily from leading positions. Gradually, this tendency increased. In the army, Red Army soldiers of Jewish origin were often removed from the award lists.

Anti-Jewish lies and clichés were spread, for example, that the Jews did not resist the German occupiers, shirked the front, and did not fight in the Red Army. After liberation, anti-Semitic incidents occurred in many places where surviving Jews returned. In Kyiv, for example, there was a full-scale pogrom in September 1945. The Soviet authorities stopped such riots, but anti-Jewish sentiments were not combated. The policy of concealing the Holocaust continued after the end of the war.

This was also demonstrated by the example of the *Black Book*, which was to document Nazi crimes against the Jewish population in the USSR. This documentation was prepared by the Jewish Anti-Fascist Committee, founded in 1942 by well-known personalities of Jewish origin. The *Black Book* was compiled under the leadership of Soviet publicist Ilya Ehrenburg and writer Vasily Grossman, and by 1946 it was ready for printing. A CC commission banned its publication. The justification for this was that the *Black Book* conveyed a "false idea of the true nature of fascism" because it gave the impression that "the Germans had fought against the USSR only with the aim of exterminating the Jews" and because there was too much reporting about collaborators and that this "weakens the responsibility that should apply to the Germans."

Nevertheless, patriotic feelings awoke in many Jewish people in the Soviet Union after the Holocaust tragedy. "Jewishness" in them was reawakened, which had been condemned in the 1920s and 1930s as a form of bourgeois nationalism. Now many Soviet Jews welcomed the establishment of the State of Israel. Golda Meir's visit to the Soviet Union in the fall of 1948 aroused great enthusiasm among them. However, when it became clear to Stalin that Israel would not follow his political goals, he intensified the anti-Semitic character of his policy. In 1948, the Jewish Anti-Fascist Committee was dissolved, and many of its members were arrested, tortured and shot. Collecting documents about the extermination of Jews became one of the main charges in a macabre way. It was now considered an attempt to select the Jews as the main victims in a nationalistic way.

The last years of Stalin's rule were accompanied by anti-Semitic campaigns, by the fight against "homeless cosmopolitans" (meaning cultural workers of Jewish origin); there were arrests of doctors (mainly of Jewish origin) accused of trying to kill Stalin and other Politburo members. No wonder that on the eve of Stalin's death, rumors circulated that Stalin was planning the deportation of Jews from major cities.

There are no monuments in Babyn Yar

After Stalin's death, the anti-Semitic course in the Soviet Union weakened somewhat. The trial of the Jewish doctors was stopped, as were the mass dismissals of Jews. During the brief thaw under Nikita Khrushchev, a number of books were published that told of the Holocaust. Among the most famous was *The Diary of Anne Frank*, which appeared in Russian translation in 1960.

Initiatives to erect monuments at the sites of mass shootings, with Jewish symbolism and inscriptions that Jews lie here, became more frequent. Such attempts had already been made after the end of the war, but in most cases, they were not permitted.

In the 1960s, a real struggle for the Babyn Yar monument unfolded. The Kyiv city authorities wanted to level Babyn Yar to build a sports stadium there. Letters of protest had no effect. Eventually, water was pumped into the gorge from a neighboring quarry as part of construction work. In March 1961, this led to a disaster: The accumulated water mixed with thawing snow and clay from a nearby brick factory. A 14-meter-high mudslide broke loose, burying numerous nearby houses and hundreds of people. This tragedy was also concealed; the dead (officially 145, recent Ukrainian research speaks of 1500 victims, editor's note) were buried secretly. An urban legend in Kyiv later interpreted the Kurenivka mudslide as punishment for disregarding the Jewish victims.

A monument in Babyn Yar was erected only in 1976, and there was no word that Jews had been shot there. Babyn Yar became a semi-banned symbol of the Holocaust because the poem "Babi Yar" by Evgeny Yevtushenko, published in 1961, triggered stormy reactions in Soviet society.

A real coming to terms with the Holocaust in the Soviet Union was hindered — albeit in a milder form than in Stalin's time — by the continuing anti-Semitic, discriminatory policy of the Soviet leadership. This was demonstrated, for example, by Khrushchev's reaction at a meeting with artists and cultural workers in March 1963, when he indicated that this topic should remain taboo. About Yevtushenko's poem, he said:

Masha Bruskina (1924–1941) and other Russian Jewish resistance fighters hanged by the Germans in Minsk on October 26, 1941. Source: Wikimedia, photographer unknown, public domain

> For what is this poetry criticized? For the fact that the author was not able to correctly portray and condemn the mass murder of the fascist criminals in Babyn Yar. In the poem it is shown as if only the Jewish population became victims of the fascist crimes, when quite a few Russians, Ukrainians and Soviet citizens of other nationalities perished at the hands of the Hitlerite executioners [...] There is no 'Jewish question,' and those who talk about such a one speak with a false voice!

Until perestroika, public remembrance of the Holocaust and Jewish resistance was effectively forbidden. Neither the Warsaw Ghetto Uprising, the Sobibor Uprising, or Jewish partisans were topics allowed by the censors.

The story of the resistance fighter Masha Bruskina, executed in Minsk in 1941 and depicted in a world-famous photograph, was significant. She was considered an unknown partisan for a long time, although her name had long been known in Minsk. Nevertheless, they did not want to mention it openly because they did not want to admit that she had been a Jew. A plaque with her name was installed in Minsk only in 2008.

In the teaching programs for schools, there was much material about the "Great Patriotic War", but the fate of Jews was hardly mentioned; all victims were simply called "peaceful Soviet citizens." The history of the Nazi concentration camps was also not associated with Jewish victims. In Soviet discourse, the most important symbol of concentration camps was not Auschwitz but Buchenwald. In the case of Buchenwald, there was no need to talk about Jews; it was possible to build a highly embellished image of international solidarity and the anti-fascist resistance struggle.

The Holocaust thus became a subject of non-conformist memory cultivated by dissidents, which, in addition to its self-identification function, became a form of resistance for many Soviet Jews. In samizdat (Ed. "self-published") the corresponding literature circulated, and local activists organized unofficial rallies at the sites of the mass shootings (at the Minsk Pit, in Babyn Yar, in Rumbula near Riga).

At the same time, tendencies to consider the Holocaust a "foreign tragedy", separate from the idea of struggle for national liberation (in Lithuania, in Ukraine), became noticeable in dissident circles.

What remains

With the end of the Soviet Union, state anti-Semitism also disappeared. It does not matter now whether one is Jewish or not, either in getting a job or a university place. The item "nationality" was removed from the identity cards of Russian citizens.

With the rejection of anti-Semitic politics, the subject of the Holocaust was also de-tabooed. As early as 1991, a scientific center for Holocaust research and Holocaust education was founded in Moscow. Films, books, and archive documents have become accessible. Even the *Black Book* could finally be published. Monuments and plaques have been erected in many places where Jews were murdered. In Moscow, the Jewish Museum has been opened, where the subject of the Holocaust has become part of the permanent exhibition.

Even now, though, this topic could not penetrate the mass consciousness. The memory of the Shoah remained suppressed for a long time, excluded from public consciousness, and banned for decades. It remains to this day not fully understood and not represented in public discourse. Coming to terms with it requires deep social reflection, refinement of historical experience, and empathy, which was and is a major problem in Russia today. Also, the great myth of the "Great Patriotic War" — which in the official discourse is presented only as a glorious victory — clouds the true picture of the war in the minds of many. The Jewish tragedy fits poorly into this picture. Jews still do not want to be recognized as victims who should die only because they were Jews. The Internet has become a haven for anti-Semites; it is enough to enter certain terms in the search engine, and there is a whole range of anti-Semitic clichés. The websites of Holocaust deniers are proliferating. Often this corresponds with the new cult of Stalin, which automatically justifies his overall policy, including the tabooing of the Holocaust in Russia.

On the other hand, the topic of the Holocaust is often used by Kremlin propaganda as a weapon against the Baltic republics and (Western) Ukraine, claiming that Nazism is being rehabilitated there and that the German occupation is being equated with the Soviet one. One takes advantage of the difficult handling of the topic in western Ukraine, Lithuania, Latvia, and Estonia, where the armed partisan resistance is heroized against the communist regime in the post-war years without any ifs and buts, and sometimes looks away when it comes to anti-Semitism and the participation of the local population in the pogroms and the persecution of the Jews.

Most notably, such propaganda cards were played in the anti-Ukrainian rhetoric against the Maidan revolution in Kyiv. Russian propaganda always claimed that anti-Semites and Bandera people who participated in the Holocaust during the war were heroized and glorified there. In this way, they try to play off the memory of communist crimes against the memory of the Holocaust.

The democratic and liberal camps should always strive to ensure that our shared tragic memories bring peoples closer together, not divide them. This goal is achievable if we succeed in sharing history.

Remembrance Must Go beyond the Concentration Camps

Nikolai Klimeniouk

There are many reasons why the Auschwitz-Birkenau concentration camp became the most important symbol of the Holocaust. With its railroad ramps, gas chambers and crematoria, with the mountains of gold teeth, hair and well-sorted personal belongings of the victims, with the sacks full of human ashes, with the unimaginably cruel medical experiments of Josef Mengele—Auschwitz thus stands for the planned, industrially managed extermination of the European Jews, for mass murder with minimal costs and maximum efficiency. This kind of murder was even more shocking because it appeared as something completely new, unprecedented, as a complete aberration of humanity.

Genocide by bullets

The Shoah also happened in a completely different way, especially on the territory of the then USSR and partly in Poland, Hungary and Romania—especially in the territories occupied by the USSR after the Hitler-Stalin Pact in 1939/40. There, a large number of European Jews were murdered, almost one million of them even before the Wannsee Conference in January 1942, but exactly how many there were, is not known to this day; Soviet victim statistics are notoriously inaccurate. It is estimated that there were up to five million Jewish people in the occupied territories of the USSR, both Soviet citizens and Jewish citizens of Poland and Hungary, who had fled and been deported; about half of them may not have survived the war. The Soviet Union did not have separate statistics of Jewish victims; they were always referred to only as "Soviet citizens." Moreover, the occupiers did not always keep accurate statistics.

Unlike in Western and Central Europe, the murder of the Jewish population in the USSR did not follow any plan, and the cost and efficiency considerations did not play any role initially. In the small town of Kamianets-Podilskyj in western Ukraine, the German occupiers shot 23,600 Jews at the end of August 1941, mostly by shooting them in the neck. This number is given in the reports by SS-Obergruppenführer Friedrich Jeckeln, who, as the highest-ranking police officer, organized the mass murder on the spot. The "Kamianets-Podilskyi massacre" is considered the first major extermination operation of the Holocaust. A month later, in the Babyn Yar ravine in Kyiv, nearly 34,000 Jews were shot in just two days. In Odesa, less than a week after the occupation of the city, Romanian troops burned approximately 25,000 Jews alive in former Red Army ammunition depots. The last two execution sites were located in the city area, and the Jewish citizens were murdered in front of their neighbors.

The consideration of hiding the killing did not play any role initially, hence the precise numbers. In the many small ghettos, as in the then-Romanian province of Transnistria, the Jewish population was simply left to starve. In the territory of today's Ukraine alone, there are about 2000 mass graves with between 500 to 2000 corpses, the vast majority of them neglected. New graves, most of which were also execution sites, are still being discovered today. Apart from Jews, Roma, Soviet prisoners of war or patients of psychiatric institutions were often murdered there, which made the statistical registration of individual victim groups even more difficult.

The Holocaust consisted not only of industrially organized mass extermination

Soviet historiography not only distracted from the targeted extermination of the Jewish population but also downplayed the involvement of the civilian population and the armies of the later satellite states of the USSR in these crimes. There were hardly any memorials to the Jewish victims, and the non-German perpetrators were not mentioned at all, if possible. This historical slander almost bordered on Holocaust denial and reverberates to this day. In the general perception of Germans, not least conveyed through history lessons, the Holocaust is, above all, industrially organized mass extermination, the main perpetrator being the National Socialist state. This optic does not reveal so clearly the role played in the Shoah by the anti-Semitism of the population in almost all European countries, by pure anti-Semitic hatred or simply by the prejudices spread long before, which only fueled the Nazis.

According to the Leipzig Authoritarianism Study published in 2018, more than 30 percent of the Germans interviewed fully or partially agree with the assertion that even today, the influence of Jews is far too great; 29 percent of respondents think Jews work more evil tricks than other people to get what they want. The mass dissemination of such prejudices contributed to the crisis of European Jewry no less than the extermination policy of the Nazi leadership.

The interpretive authority over victims and perpetrators

On the other hand, today's Russian historical policy emphasizes the collaboration of the Ukrainian or Polish population in Nazi crimes beyond any measure. Ukraine and Poland, even in liberal circles, are portrayed less as victims and more as accomplices of German Nazi crimes. Very symptomatic of this was the outrage campaign staged by the Kremlin on the eve of the anniversary of the liberation of Auschwitz in 2015. The Kremlin claimed Poland had not invited Russian President Vladimir Putin out of pure "Russophobia," while Russia was the rightful representative of the Soviet Union, which had liberated Auschwitz. This assertion contained several untruths. The commemoration was not an act of state; the organizer, the Auschwitz Memorial, did not send out invitations to attend but accepted registrations, including from heads of state.

The Soviet Union did indeed liberate Auschwitz, but the liberation was not really planned. According to his later memoirs, the commander of the unit that was the first to advance to the concentration camp, Major Anatoly Shapiro, did not even know of the camp's existence: Soviet maps showed only forest at that location. The person of commander also caused wild speculations. The Jewish officer was born in Ukraine and spent almost all his life there until he emigrated to the USA in 1992. Ukraine was represented at the memorial service. In Ukraine, Shapiro is celebrated as a hero; in 2006, for example, then-President Viktor Yushchenko posthumously awarded him the country's highest decoration. In Russia, it was alleged that Ukraine wanted to claim the achievement of the entire USSR for itself and thus distract attention from the crimes of Ukrainian nationalists (in official Russian parlance, "Bandera fascists"). It was also heard from Russia that the state of Poland had built the Auschwitz concentration camp and was now humiliating Russia by not inviting the head of state.

In the years that followed, this rhetoric intensified. Vladimir Putin's two speeches in Jerusalem on January 23, 2020, one at the memorial ceremony in Yad Vashem and the other at the opening of the memorial to the victims of the blockade of Leningrad, sounded very much in this vein: the collaborators from Ukraine, Poland, Lithuania and Latvia had been even worse, even crueler than their "German masters," and they, in turn, had planned the same fate, annihilation, for the Russians and other Slavic peoples.

These disputes make it clear that the Second World War is obviously not a closed chapter in history. Today, its horrors are increasingly instrumentalized for current political purposes. When we commemorate the victims of the Holocaust, we must not lose sight of those who fell victim to unveiled violence in Eastern Europe. People, not the soulless and faceless state, murdered their fellow Jews. The anti-Semitism of Europeans was as responsible for the Shoah as the policies of the Nazis. For this European, anti-Semitism is anything but dead.

Forced Laborers from Ukraine
Destiny and Memory

Gelinada Grinchenko

"The typical Ostarbeiter came from Ukraine, was female and 18 years old." Such was the formula of words that once accompanied the traveling documentary exhibition entitled *A Crack in Life. Memories of Ukrainian forced laborers in the Rhineland*. The project concerned the destinies of Ukrainian women whose lives were profoundly marked by years of forced labor in Nazi Germany, leaving indelible wounds. More than that, these years were a turning point in their lives because after the evils, humiliations and the disbelief of a stranger on returning home, normal life no longer existed for them. The formerly enslaved people could expect childless lives, unhappiness, sometimes late and short marriages, scornful attitudes in their youth and loneliness in their old age. The exhibition recounted the stories of only ten women forced to work in the Land of Rhineland. However, the number of those removed from Ukraine during the war, not only women but also men, old, young, and even children, was more than two and a half million.

These people were known as *Ostarbeiters* [workers from the East]. They made up the largest and one of the most discriminated groups of civilian workers. The Third Reich employed more than 8 million during the war. The Nazis used a humiliating definition for workers of non German nationality, *Volkszugehörigkeit* [ethnic origin], recruited in the Reichskomissariat of Ukraine, the General Commissariat of Belarus, and in the regions located east of these commissariats. The Wehrmacht removed them from the occupied territories to the Third Reich to perform forced labor. The widespread use of civilian workers from Ukraine lasted from the beginning of 1942 to the beginning of 1945. In the territory of the German Reich, they worked in all fields and spheres where forced labor of foreigners was introduced: in the processing and manufacturing industries, transport and construction, agriculture, home, municipal, church, and so forth.

The first orders regarding the treatment of workers from the East and the rules for their care were extremely strict. During the recruitment process, Soviet workers had to undergo a medical examination, which was frequently no more than superficial, as the workers later mentioned: "They have hands and feet—good!" They were transported to Germany in closed cars ("as livestock, standing, almost without food and water.") They were unloaded for work at special points where their muscles were felt; they looked into their mouths and checked their teeth. The *Ostarbeiters* had to work mainly in closed brigades, isolated from German and other foreign workers, only in rural areas. The first workers from Ukraine had to live in closed, barbed-wire camps, in barracks and were not to go anywhere or communicate with anyone.

The living conditions in the camps varied and often depended on the factory management to which they were attached and the head of the camp itself. The managers, with certain exceptions, were almost uninterested in the daily lives of the *Ostarbeiters*, who worked up to 18 hours a day. In large farms, enslaved Ukrainians also worked from dawn to dusk, often living together with or alongside cattle. They were beaten, abused, and forced to work to the point of exhaustion. From the middle of 1942, due to the growing needs of the German military economy for labor, as well as the need to increase the efficiency of the use of the "labor from the East", certain measures were introduced to ease the lives and improve the living and working conditions of Ukrainian workers. These measures were introduced throughout the last three years of forced labor in the Reich. However, these improvements often remained only on paper, and the conditions of the *Ostarbeiters* continued to be extremely precarious. The *Ostarbeiters* were often left to their own devices since they were not considered people but eastern production tools which could easily be replaced. Even the German inspectorates who inspected the *Ostarbeiter* camps wrote in 1943 that the forced laborers were incredibly exhausted, the mood was terrible, the camps dirty, and the food insufficient. However, the *Ostarbeiters* were very patient, and these inspectors continued. They work until they fall face down in the mud right there at the workplace, but no one treats them, all the doctor can do is issue a death certificate.

After mid-1942, *Ostarbeiters* were officially allowed censored correspondence. Despite this, a certain number of their letters and leaflets escaped German censorship and arrived at their destination unverified. It was from these letters that relatives learned about food insufficiencies, black market speculation, eating raw vegetable leaves, theft of potatoes and logs, leading to subsequent harsh punishments, cold and lousy barracks, lack of clothes and shoes, unsatisfactory medical care, etc.

While Ukrainian civilians remained in Germany working for the Reich, their lives were blighted not only by exhausting work, hunger, and precarious living conditions but also by various diseases. The main illnesses were exhaustion and cardiovascular diseases, tuberculosis, lung inflammation, gastrointestinal diseases, and typhoid fever epidemics. Attempts at self-mutilation or self-infection were common amongst the camps where the *Ostarbeiters* lived, but they often ended tragically. Those who initiated collective self-infection were demonstrably punished or sent to concentration camps.

A separate group of young people taken from Ukraine was young women forced to work in German households. In September 1942, a decree was issued requiring the provision to Germany of half a million female *Ostarbeiters* aged 15–35. They had to be of strong stature and, if possible, resemble German women in their outer appearance (blue eyes and blond hair). For example, in one month alone (from mid-October to mid-November), 3,143 young women were sent from the territory of Kharkiv and outlying regions to work on German farms. With rare exceptions when the young Ukrainian girls were treated calmly and respectfully by the German family, the work of these maids was accompanied by shouting, beating and humiliation. The young girls would collapse with exhaustion due to the heavy labor, which included washing piles of dishes, washing windows, laundering and ironing linens, sewing and repairing clothes and household items, chopping firewood, working in the yard, and much more.

However, the most incredible and inhumane aspect was the use of child labor and bullying of young children who were also taken to Germany during the war. The Ukrainian children came to Germany mainly with their families. If they were physically strong, they would be employed in agriculture, and after the end of 1943, they were made to help remove debris after air raids. Rules required that children over 14 years of age should work no more than 4 hours a day. After the end of 1943, the age limit was lowered to 10, and the 4-hour limit on child labor ceased to apply after May 1944. The children of the *Ostarbeiters* were used to working almost everywhere where the forced labor of citizens of the occupied territories had been introduced: in industry, agriculture, utilities and services, on construction and railways. The use of children from the age of 7 was used particularly on the railways.

This dreadful fear would remain with them for the rest of their lives, the fear that only a child can experience, the fear of losing their family, the fear of losing their mother. Inesa Mirchevska, a Kyivan, in her book *And My Birthday Present From Him was My Mother: A Confession* wrote of the incredible trials she had to experience as a little girl. Little Inesa was sent into forced labor at the age of 10 with her mother. She lived with her for a while in a work camp and worked with other children in the kitchen. One day, after a commission visited the camp to look at the children, quite clearly making preparations for their removal, Inesa's mother refused to go to work. She remained with her daughter to prevent her removal. For this disobedience, the mother was imprisoned in a punishment cell and sentenced to execution in the morning. The woman was led to a gallows in the presence of all the camp inmates, including little Inesa. Suddenly, a woman approached the commandant and said something to him. The following is a quote:

> He called me over (I already understood German quite well). I went up to him. The commandant asked if it was true that it was my 11th birthday today. I answered. And he so said, "Today's your birthday!" He thought for a moment. Then he shouted something to the men who were dragging my mummy. They went over to him. He examined my mother from head to toe and said, "Your mother broke the camp rules. I have to punish her severely, and I was going to do that, but... You are 11 today, is that right? Today is your birthday. I have had a rather original idea: I'll give you a gift... I'll give

you an expensive and original gift. I don't think anyone has ever received one like it before!... And he gave me my mummy. My dear, darling mummy. We rushed to each other, hugged, kissed, stroked, touched each other. We were allowed to go to the barracks. Mummy was covered in bruises. I clenched my fists, but what could I do? He could execute and he could show mercy. And he had shown mercy. It was purely his whim, his will....

Along with the memory of the tragedies and calamities of the war years, the hearts of former *Ostarbeiters* also retain the memory of the dearest and most important thing in life — friendship, help, sincere and open love impassioned in defiance of war, freedom, age, language and cultural barriers. After the collapse of the USSR, when they could speak out with a full voice, many memories of the formerly enslaved people of the Third Reich were published in Ukraine, hundreds of their spoken stories were recorded, performances were staged, and special museum exhibitions were held. The memory of these enslaved people is immortalized in monuments and memorial plaques. Books have been written about them, and documentary films have been made. Many such memorial initiatives have also involved German partners. However, in Germany, very little is known about the fate of the Ukrainian *Ostarbeiters*. Their memory is perpetuated in countless memorial signs locally or in individual museums subjects and exhibitions. Such commemorative signs have appeared in the main thanks to local grassroots initiatives, school or student projects, and the work of historical workshops, etc. However, these memorial initiatives often refer to workers from Ukraine as Russians or Soviet people, and their total number, including those who died in captivity and have remained forever in a foreign land, remains unidentified.

Establishing the names and the exact number of Ukrainians killed in captivity, pinpointing their burial places and erecting monuments, commemorating all the victims of slave labor by installing memorial plaques in their places of work or detention, translating and publishing the memoirs and oral stories of the former *Ostarbeiters* are some of the keyways of preserving and disseminating the memory of the lives of the Ukrainian *Ostarbeiters*. Over all the years of searching for ways to commemorate the experience of forced labor during National Socialism, the memory of this very phenomenon (which is still rare in modern European discourses on the Second World War) has revealed not conflict but a tangible potential for reconciliation and understanding. It is for this reason that the dissemination of knowledge and the perpetuation of the memory of forced workers from Ukraine, who made up a predominant majority of all the *Ostarbeiters*, has contributed and will continue to contribute to the search for mutual understanding and to establish contacts between people and countries, dialogue between generations, and the study and preservation of knowledge about the tragic events and trials of the Second World War, one of which was forced labor.

Sources

Grinchenko, G.: *Usna istrorija prymusu do praci: metod, konteksty, teksty*, "HTMT", Kharkiv 2012.

Herbert, U.: *Fremdarbeiter: Politik und Praxis des 'Ausländer-Einsatzes' in der Kriegswirtschaft des Dritten Reiches*, Dietz, Bonn 1999.

Mirzcewskaja, I. B.: *I on podaril mne mamu: vospominania*, KMS "Poesia", 2005.

Polian, P.: *Zhertvy dvukh dyktatur: zhizn, trud, unizhenija i smert sovetskikh vojennopliennykh i ostarbaiterov na cuzhbinie i rodinie*, ROSSPEN, Moskau 2002.

Spoerer, M.: *Zwangsarbeit unter dem Hakenkreuz. Ausländische Zivilarbeiter, Kriegsgefangene und Häftlinge im Deutsche Reich und im besetzten Europa 1939-1945*, Deutsche Verlagsanstalt, Stuttgart/München 2001.

The Ukrainian Image of the Germans
Thoughts on a Tragedy

Sebastian Christ

For a not inconsiderable number of Germans, Ukraine exists only on the map, although it was the target of the worst German delusions and the scene of some of the most atrocious crimes. For these Germans, Ukraine is not a place of special historical responsibility but rather a territory created by a whim of history, devoid of characteristics and incapable of its own action.

And because in a territory, it is not the people living there but the space in the foreground of perception, the debate about Ukraine is rarely about Ukrainians and their wishes but rather about claims to dominion and power over their land mass. When people talk about Ukraine, they like to talk about it in "geopolitical" terms. The people of Ukraine are far too rarely perceived as actors in world history.

All this is not a coincidence but a product of German colonialism in Eastern Europe, which has been denied until now. In principle, this affects all states that lie between Germany's eastern and Russia's western borders. However, the Baltic States and the Visegrád States have been part of the European Union for over fifteen years. Especially in the case of Poland, it is possible to observe how old prejudices are slowly dissolving: Harald Schmidt's racist jokes about lazy and thieving Poles, which were still considered entertaining on German television in the late 1990s, would be unthinkable today.

The situation is different in Ukraine. The grandchildren feel surprisingly little empathy for this part of Europe, where the German grandparent generation once wanted to conquer "living space in the East" and kill millions of people. Moreover, even the grandchildren still cultivate central motifs of the German colonial ambitions in Eastern Europe — possibly without being aware of it. For the Germans' "coming to terms with the past" has so far not gone beyond the Carpathians. Nowhere is this more evident than when talking about Ukraine. Five thoughts on this.

First: Parts of the German public deny Ukraine's statehood

Take Richard David Precht, for example. The philosopher and book author likes to be asked when it comes to classifying current developments. In 2017, he invited ex-general Harald Kujat, who now works for the Kremlin-affiliated think tank Dialogue of Civilizations, to his ZDF show to talk about the topic of "wars." In the course of NATO's eastward expansion, Precht said, Russia had been deprived of "countries of influence." In 2013, he said, only "the very little Georgia, the desolate Belarus and the little Ukraine" remained for Russia.

Moreover, Precht said he could not understand why Ukraine had actually been given hope of joining the EU because: "Let's think about how many destitute people would have come to Europe from this famine-stricken country. What could the Ukrainians have sold us?" By accepting Ukraine, the EU would have created a "construction site" that would have been "a hundred times bigger than Greece."

Ukraine as "Russia's country of influence" whose "destitute" people are just waiting to move to the rich states of Western Europe — Precht manages here miraculously to present Ukraine twice as a territory. On the one hand, as a country to which the great power Russia has a right of access and disposal — just as if Ukraine were a colony. On the other hand, as a country whose most striking characteristic is the push factors against its own population. Precht understands Ukraine as a space that people would rather leave than shape. And Ukrainians would immediately trade their homeland for the promise of hard currency.

This view of Eastern Europe, which is as colonialist as it is racist, has a very long tradition in Germany. In 1862, the Prussian historian Heinrich von Treitschke formulated a very influential hypothesis in his work *Das Deutsche Ordensland Preußen* [Prussia, the German Order Land]: According to this hypothesis, Germany, as the bearer of high culture, was capable of founding a state, whereas countries like Poland were not. "Every day, Germans still carry the blessing of culture to the East. But in the Slavic country the German teacher is received sullenly as an impudent intruder," Treitschke wrote.

Von Treitschke was not alone with such ideas. The writer Gustav Freytag wrote in his novel *Soll und Haben* [Debit and Credit] as early as 1855: "There is no race which has so little what it takes to get ahead and acquire humanity and education through capital as the Slavic." The book was a bestseller for many decades and, among other things, shaped the image of the "Polish economy" — the alleged inability of the Slavs to organize themselves and build wealth — that was common until the 20th century. In the empire, denying Poland and other Slavic nations statehood was consensual. This widespread hostility to Slavs, in turn, made it easy for the Nazis to legitimize their excesses on the territory of Ukraine. If people are incapable of statehood, their land can be colonized and plundered.

Such ideas resonate. To this day, it seems neither offensive nor absurd to the German public when, for example, the Ukrainian national emblem is referred to as a "Nazi symbol". In fact, this is exactly what the Bundestag faction of the Left Party did in an official press release in the fall of 2014. Here, too, a circle is perfidiously closed in that the descendants of the former National Socialist colonial power accuse the descendants of the victims of preferring to identify themselves as a Nazi successor state rather than as a Ukrainian democracy — and no one in Germany contradicts them.

Second: Where there is no state of its own, there are no politically active people either

The ZDF satirical program *Die Anstalt* made Ukraine the topic of discussion several times in 2014 without addressing Ukraine itself. The country always served as a projection screen for seemingly perfidious plans or conspiracy theories. In March 2014, for example, cabaret artist Max Uthoff suggested in a four-minute segment that the West was planning a war against Russia, that Western countries had supported the Maidan to promote arms exports, and that the

West was trying to instrumentalize Ukraine as a "new, globalized shopping mall" through the IMF.

In this view, Ukraine becomes a playing field of foreign, powerful actors. The people of Ukraine do not have their own dreams, desires and fears, which may have led to intrinsically motivated protests. Following this thinking, the Ukrainian people are only an instrument of world politics. For a long time, for example, the conspiracy theory persisted in Germany that the CIA had "bought" the Maidan in order to bring about "regime change." To this day, the AfD (Alternative for Germany party) in the Bundestag cannot decide whether the US is the "determining force" in Ukraine or whether the election of Volodymyr Zelenskyy as Ukrainian president will lead to what it sees as a welcome rapprochement with Russia.

At the same time, reducing Ukraine to an available territory in the struggle between Russia and the Western world is by no means a legitimate political idea and certainly not an innocent one. It implies that world politics can be made with Ukraine—but without Ukrainians. The removal of the human from the political sphere that this implies sometimes reverberates in the form of psychotic notions of fear in the discourse in Germany.

For example, at the so-called 'Berlin Monday Vigils' in 2014, the far-right publicist Jürgen Elsässer spread the thesis that NATO was planning the "final solution to the Russian question" with the conflict in Ukraine and was aiming for a war of aggression. For this, he received applause from thousands of demo participants as the burning fear of a war with Russia was, in fact, the most important thing that interested many Germans in the conflict in Ukraine at the beginning of 2014.

Third: Many Germans see Russia as the only Eastern European state on an equal footing

Ukraine has been the target of imperial politics several times in its history. Tsars, Soviet leaders and Nazis tried to make policies at the expense of the Ukrainian people and their identity.

Moreover, one of the many tragedies of the Ukrainian present is that the imperial powers of the past still fight their imperial battles. The conflicts of that time live on under different auspices.

Sometimes this shows up in small things: In 2015, for example, cabaret artist Volker Pispers repeatedly claimed that "27 million Russian soldiers" had died in World War II and that Russia had never invaded "the West." He used this argument, of all things, to criticize Germany's policy toward Russia after the outbreak of war in eastern Ukraine. Perhaps Pispers really did not know that it was 27 million Soviet citizens who died in World War II—including many millions of people from Ukraine and Belarus. Perhaps he really had no idea that in 1939 the Soviet Union, with Nazi Germany's approval, invaded eastern Poland (including what is now western Ukraine), Bessarabia and the Baltic states. On the other hand, apparently, no one from his environment pointed this out to him.

The repetition of old conflicts sometimes shows up on a large scale: In December 2014, *Die Zeit* published an appeal entitled "War again in Europe? Not in our name!" The text appeared nine months after Russia's annexation of Crimea and three months after the intervention of regular Russian troops in the Battle of Ilovaisk led to the deaths of hundreds of Ukrainian soldiers. The authors lamented the West's "eastward expansion, which seems threatening to Russia," criticized Western media for their reporting and called for a new policy of détente with Russia. The appeal was signed by German President Roman Herzog, German Chancellor Gerhard Schröder, journalist Gabriele Krone-Schmalz and prominent cultural figures such as director Wim Wenders and actor Mario Adorf. Ukraine did not appear as an actor in this text. Most importantly, the war in eastern Ukraine was not mentioned. It was remarkable: more than sixty German politicians and celebrities, some very well-known, warned against war, although Russia had already triggered a war for a long time. The fear of a confrontation with Russia was evidently so great that these important Germans discussed the existing war in eastern Ukraine, which at that time had already claimed several thousand lives, as if it did not exist.

Many Germans generally tend not to see themselves in relation to supposedly weaker or smaller states but in relation to the major orienting powers of world politics. This, too, is a legacy of past imperial politics. The US and Russia can polarize public discourse in Germany because they are seen as powers on an equal footing.

In April 2014, just a few weeks after the annexation of Crimea in violation of international law, Infratest dimap published a survey on the political self-perception of Germans. Barack Obama was still the US president at the time. Despite this, only 45 percent wanted to maintain the old westward commitment of German foreign policy, while 49 percent favored a "middle position" for Germany between the US and Russia. Germany was so busy trying to fit into the concert of the greats that Ukraine became again what it had always been—just a territory in German thinking about politics.

Fourth: We Germans have been silent about the crimes against the Ukrainians for so long that today we lack the words, images and symbols to do justice to this historical responsibility.

Breaking down colonial thought patterns can only be achieved by dealing with colonialism itself. And here, Germany is still at the very beginning. This is also because the arguments in the discourse on colonialism and racism are currently mostly imported from the Anglophone cultural area.

If, for example, it is said in the US that there is no racism against people of white skin color, then this is an accurate statement in relation to US social conditions. However, suppose one relates this argument to Germany and German history. In that case, it remains completely incomprehensible why the National Socialists wanted to murder about a quarter of the Ukrainian population in World War II for racist reasons—as stated in the General Plan East. Large parts of Eastern Europe were to become settler colonies. In addition, nearly 4.4 million civilian forced laborers from Poland and the Soviet Union were enslaved during World War II and taken to Germany.

Some Germans find it equally difficult to understand that the colonial policies of European imperial powers were not exclusive to Asia and Africa. Journalist and migration researcher Mark Terkessidis believes that German crimes against the Slavic population of Eastern Europe did not fit into the "two schemes of memory that have become global," namely the memory of the Holocaust, focusing on the extermination of European Jews and the memory of slavery and colonialism, focusing on people of color. As a result, Eastern European experiences with Nazi occupation policies could often only be validated through references to the Holocaust.

The Holocaust and the German colonial policy in Eastern Europe are indeed closely connected. Why the Holocaust became possible only becomes clear when we understand why Hitler invaded the Soviet Union in 1941. Timothy Snyder had already made this clear in a speech to the Green Party's parliamentary group in the Bundestag in 2017. "If Hitler had not had the colonialist idea of waging a war in Eastern Europe to control Ukraine," Snyder said, "there could not have been the Holocaust." For it was this plan of living space in the East that expanded the German sphere of power into Eastern Europe, where millions of Jewish people lived, he said. And it was only after the beginning of the occupation in Ukraine, with the cruel massacres of Kamianets-Podilskyi and Babyn Jar, that it became clear that something like the Holocaust was even possible.

"What does that mean?" asked Snyder at the time. "It means that every German who takes seriously the idea of responsibility for the Holocaust must also take seriously the history of the German occupation of Ukraine."

The truth is, however, that we simply lack the words, images and symbols to do justice to this historical responsibility. And that is why we also do not have the necessary categories to talk about the consequences of what happened for our present and what it does to us today.

Fifth: Ukraine has too few advocates in Germany

But how do we start to find concepts? Where will the images and symbols come from that will make it easier for us to speak? How do we get Ukraine to be seen not just as a territory but as a country whose place in our own historical identity we not only know but also feel?

Some beginnings give us hope. One of the most remarkable European stories since 2014 is that Ukraine has built up something like cultural soft power. Before the outbreak of the coronavirus crisis, for example, Kyiv was one of Europe's hottest city break destinations. Vyshyvanka fashion has enjoyed worldwide success, musicians such as the singer Jamala are perceived against the backdrop of their specifically Ukrainian history, and more and more international institutions are using the Ukrainian-language spelling for the capital, which used to be transliterated as "Kiev." The "Revolution of Dignity" has not only helped to shape a new image of the Ukrainian nation internally but has also added several new facets to Ukraine's image abroad. The image of Ukraine in Germany is slowly taking shape.

However, it is also true that the Ukrainian state has so far made surprisingly little of this new communicability of its own nation. Ukraine should actually be much more interested in actively presenting itself in Germany. Russia, for example, is still much more adept at addressing young elites in Germany and elsewhere in Europe and also promoting them through various institutions. And cultural exchange is also so important that it could use more support. Wouldn't it be conceivable, for example, to set up a financing fund to translate Ukrainian literature into German or English? What about a more intensive German-Ukrainian youth exchange program that would help to familiarize schoolchildren, pupils and students with Ukraine?

There are not yet enough prominent Germans in politics, culture and academia to give a voice to Ukraine's interests. Above all, however, Ukraine lacks a presence in the everyday lives of Germans. And because this is the case, there is also a lack of the necessary knowledge that makes sociopolitical change possible in the first place.

The reception of history and the anticipation of the future are subject to similar social negotiation processes. If we lack the necessary concepts, we may be unable to describe the past as it is for us today. Likewise, we cannot develop possible visions of the future if our subjective knowledge of the present is inadequate and does not do justice to the future.

Precisely for this reason, it can be a worthwhile adventure to expand our historical awareness and fill Ukraine's "blank space" with knowledge. In the end, a view of Ukraine could emerge that is free of historically inherited disparagement — and that allows us to see the opportunities and the potentials that in a common future.

Was Ukraine a Colony?

Gerhard Simon

Ukraine has been an independent nation-state (only) since 1991, a disintegration product of the Soviet Union like all the fifteen former Union republics, including Russia. On the other hand, Ukraine has a history of more than a thousand years. Kyiv was the center of the first East Slavic state formation; the Christianization of the East Slavs — Russians, Ukrainians and Belarusians — began here. However, there was no uninterrupted state continuity. Attempts to form an independent state failed in the seventeenth century and at the beginning of the twentieth century after the First World War.

The Empire as Anti-Imperium

So, what was Ukraine in the late Tsarist Empire and the Soviet Union: a loose bunch of provinces belonging to different states? A colony? In its self-representation, the Soviet Union rejected far from its mind the idea that the USSR was an empire like any other. More than that, the perception of the Soviet Union as an "anti-empire" was also widely accepted in the West. Soviet ideology and propaganda succeeded in marketing the Soviet system as overcoming and liberating from colonialism.

In the communist narrative, therefore, there could be no Soviet colonies. Today — more than a quarter of a century after the end of the Soviet Union — the self perception in the former Union republics has turned into the opposite: Everywhere, the colonial legacy from Russian and Soviet times is lamented with more or less emphasis, and decolonization is demanded and practiced. With one exception: Russia. Even in Belarus, the most Sovietized and Russified republic, where a massive protest movement was forming from below in 2020, opposition forces are calling for overcoming the colonial past. Three of the five Central Asian states (Uzbekistan since 1995, Turkmenistan since 1993, and Kazakhstan since 2017) are even discarding Cyrillic letters and adopting Latin ones.

Soviet colonialism

No doubt, Soviet colonialism had its peculiarities and differed from British, French and other colonial empires, this favored mimicry. In addition: The Bolsheviks had been victorious in the Civil War after 1917 because they promised to open the "tsarist prison of nations" and release the non-Russian peoples into freedom and state independence. They did not keep their promise, but the Ukrainian nation and many others got their own Soviet republic. Ukrainian language and culture were promoted, and Russian was pushed back. Early Soviet nationality policy differed massively and positively from the late Tsarist Empire when even the name Ukraine was banned. Stalin, however, withdrew many concessions in the 1930s; no Ukrainian national communist survived 1939.

However, the facade of Soviet federalism remained, and it was by no means meaningless. It was only outside the Soviet Union, especially in Germany, that both before and after 1945, it was customary to perceive only the Russians in the Soviet Union and to forget the Ukrainians and other nationalities — that is, half of the population; Soviet Russia was considered an unofficial state designation in the Federal Republic of Germany.

With the Soviet Union, the Russian Empire returned to the map in a new form. The Bolsheviks tightened and refined the central elements of imperial rule, whose goal was the subjugation of the colonies. The centralization of all important and many unimportant decisions in Moscow remained the general line of the Communist Party until the end of the Soviet Union, and its strictly hierarchical structure guaranteed the maintenance of imperial rule. Although Ukraine and the other Union republics (according to Soviet reading) had their own statehood, power-sharing with Moscow or negotiating competencies between the metropolis and the colonies was out of the question. In this respect, Soviet federalism was the opposite of federalism in the Western democratic understanding.

But who was the metropolis in the Soviet empire? The Russian people as a whole were neither rulers nor beneficiaries of the empire in tsarist nor Soviet times. Power was held by the leading apparatuses and officials of the Communist Party, the armed forces, the security services, the state apparatus, and the business community (the so-called nomenklatura). Although Russians formed a disproportionate majority of this power elite, it also included numerous non-Russians, including many Ukrainians.

Ukraine as a colony

Ukraine had no independent decision-making authority, not only in politics but also in economics and culture. Although the country had been a member of the United Nations since 1945, there was no foreign policy independent of Moscow. As early as the 1920s, Ukrainian economists publicly complained about the country's colonial dependence on Moscow. It was only there that decisions on the distribution of investments were made. A common thread throughout the Soviet period was the Ukrainian claim that the country paid more into the general budget than it received back. Thus, Ukraine was the Union's paymaster. Until the end, the only way for Kyiv to influence economic policy decisions at the central office was through unofficial lobbying or corruption of the metropolis. This was used extensively and not without success.

While Ukraine enjoyed wide latitude in the area of culture in the early Soviet period, freedom of movement, in particular, became increasingly restricted in the last 25 years of the Soviet Union. Moscow decided in which universities and schools Russian or Ukrainian was the language of instruction or how many books could be published in Ukrainian.

In addition to colonization imposed and enforced from above, there was self-colonization in anticipatory obedience. Long-established patterns of behavior dating back to tsarist times, experience with the terror of the Stalin era, and fear of an uncertain future have made forming an independent European identity in Ukraine more difficult and fostered inferiority complexes. It fits well into this picture that, on the other hand, there were and are radical nationalist groups for whom Ukraine is "above everything."

Decolonization

Parallel to colonization, processes of decolonization already took place in the Soviet period; these included, in particular, the emergence of national, non-Russian elites who increasingly claimed their republics for themselves and made the Russian elite superfluous. These processes made the Ukrainian nation significantly more tightly knit and capable of action at the end of the Soviet period than after the First World War. Thus, contrary to its intentions, Soviet nationality policy did not lead to the "merging" of nations but contributed to their independence.

The contradictory nature of developments in the last Soviet decades prepared the break at the end of perestroika: On the one hand, the self-confidence of the new Ukrainian elites grew vis-à-vis Moscow, as they were no longer dependent on "big brother"; on the other hand, the metropolis tried to counteract with petty paternalism in language and cultural policy. The simultaneity of the uneven processes of nation-building and colonization ultimately led to an explosive mixture that contributed significantly to the collapse of the Soviet Union.

Today there is a broad consensus among the Ukrainian public that decolonization is an irreversible but incomplete process; setbacks are considered conceivable. The country has come a long way from the metropolis since 1991, culturally as well as in domestic and foreign policy, and has made great strides on the road from object to subject of international politics.

Russia's Postcolonial War on Ukraine

One of the main threats to Ukrainian independence is that Russia does not recognize the loss of empire and has been waging a postcolonial war against Ukraine since 2014 with the aim of either returning Ukraine to hegemonic dependence on what is now called the "Russian world" or turning it into a *failed state*, or in any case preventing the integration of a free Ukraine into the European community of states. These Russian positions also have supporters in Ukraine, albeit—as shown by polls and the elections of recent years—with a clearly declining tendency. The war in the Donbas has contributed to the fact that the advocates of reintegration with Russia as an alternative to Europe now represent a small minority.

Chernobyl — Chornobyl
A Place of Remembrance of Global Significance

Anna Veronika Wendland

There is a *Chernobyl* and a *Chornobyl*. *Chernobyl* is a place of memory in the world memory of modernity, a landmark in the Anthropocene, and the most serious nuclear accident in the history of civilian nuclear energy. *Chornobyl* is a Ukrainian country town at the mouth of the Ush River into the Pripyat River, located about one hundred kilometers north of Kyiv in the Polissia forest and swamp landscape.

Until the last third of the twentieth century, Chornobyl lay in the slipstream of history. Even long after the dawn of the railroad age, the place was accessible only by ship for a long time. The Jewish-Ukrainian shtetl was considered something especially among Hasidic pious people because it was the seat of a famous Torah scholarly family. This old Chornobyl, where Jews, Ukrainians, Polish and German minorities had lived house to house, as in countless other places in Ukraine, was already hit hard in the 1930s by Stalinist purges and the consequences of forced collectivization. Its final demise was sealed between November 1941 and the end of 1942 by the German occupiers, who murdered the entire Jewish population of the town and its surrounding area in two shooting campaigns.

In the late 1960s, the new Chornobyl emerged, now as the vanishing point of progress-euphoric reporting in major Soviet newspapers. Ukraine's first nuclear power plant was to be built near the district town, one of the most powerful in the world at the time. Chornobyl, the town, lent its name to Chernobyl, the power plant, which was thus also immediately Russified but remained further away. The future was being built 18 kilometers to the north in the form of the huge nuclear plant and the modern nuclear engineering town of Pripyat, built on the banks of the river of the same name. In 1977, the first unit went online.

Unlike in Germany, nuclear energy was unchallenged in Soviet Ukraine before 1986. The country was on a modernization path. Education- and advancement-hungry Ukrainians began streaming out of starved and war-ravaged villages in the late 1950s and into the cities, where Khrushchev's economic miracle promised jobs and housing. Ukrainian party and scientific elites welcomed nuclear power and actively sought opportunities for Ukrainian participation in the all-Soviet process of civilian nuclearization. As much nuclear expertise as possible was to be concentrated in energy-hungry Ukraine. And indeed, as in many other fields, Ukraine was something of a *secunda inter pares* in the Soviet nuclear state. Not only were there renowned research institutes and universities here that supplied the emerging nuclear industry with specialists, but the nuclear elites of the Soviet Union also came to a large extent from Ukraine. They were presided over by a Ukrainian, Yuchym (Yefim) Slavsky, the all-powerful ruler of the nuclear military-industrial complex, the minister of "medium engineering," a code name for reactor construction and nuclear fuel cycle. The engineer and descendant of an eastern Ukrainian Cossack family had one of the Soviet nuclear cities in Kazakhstan named after the Ukrainian national poet Taras Shevchenko out of patriotic nostalgia because he had lived nearby in tsarist exile. Incidentally, like most Ukrainians in imperial career positions, he staunchly represented the Moscow line. This line also included a regime of strict obedience that made self-criticism and discussing errors in the Soviet nuclear energy industry impossible.

Locally, too, nuclear power was welcomed. The decision-makers in Kyiv knew that the coal era, with its depleting reserves in the Donbas, was past its prime; the use of hydropower had been exhausted with the almost continuous regulation of the Dnipro. But the newly settled industry, growing cities and mechanized agriculture needed electricity. Nuclear energy appeared safe and clean in contrast to the tremendous pollution and devastation in the heavy industrial areas. Soviet propaganda presented the Chernobyl NPP as a techno idyll in a pristine natural landscape where academically educated, white-clad specialists did their duty. The peaceful atom knew only success stories. The people of Prypiat considered themselves lucky to live in a privileged city where one did not have to wait as long for housing as the average Soviet citizen.

Chornobyl before Chernobyl: In the 1970s, nuclear energy became part of everyday life for many Ukrainians who lived and worked in nuclear towns like Prypiat. After the accident, the evacuated Pripyat residents revived their town in digital archives. Electrician Ivan Zholud provided his private photo albums; shown here is a photo of his children on a trip to units 3 and 4 of the nuclear power plant that later crashed in December 1983. Source: Ivan Zholud, Prypiat-city.ru

At the same time, nuclear cities like Prypiat were being built in other parts of Ukraine. Their citizens were proud to work in high-tech plants and to supply their country with electricity without covering it in black smoke. Many private photo archives of Chernobyl nuclear workers, which were made accessible to a wider public on memorial websites after the accident, bear witness to this pride — and to the everyday life of living with the atom.

The dream of a clean, nature-compatible atom was shattered on the night of April 26, 1986. A functional test on the electrical equipment of the fourth, newest unit in the power plant brought the plant out of control through an unfortunate chain of circumstances. A nuclear power excursion destroyed the reactor along with the surrounding building. The highly radioactive reactor inventory dispersed with the air currents of an early summer large-scale weather situation over the whole of Europe, later the entire Northern Hemisphere. The accident thus became a global catastrophe. Far from Ukraine, it triggered political upheavals because governments and scientists had no clear answers to the questions and concerns of the population in the face of a transboundary, uncertain threat. As the "GAU of expert culture" (Joachim Radkau), Chernobyl highlighted the alienation between scientific and technical elites and an increasingly distrustful population in Western industrial societies. The nuclear accident spurred the rise of the Green Party as a major political force in Germany and laid the axe to the German nuclear energy industry. The center of the accident in Ukraine was soon no longer even mentioned.

On the ground, unlike in Germany, the outcome of the Chernobyl accident was indeed devastating. More than fifty people died in agony from acute radiation sickness in the first days and weeks after the accident. Most of them were power plant employees, first responders and firefighters, whose selfless efforts presumably prevented far worse. As a late consequence, the WHO expects about 4000 premature deaths from cancer. An area of 2600 square kilometers in the northwest of the Kyiv administrative district, which, together with extensive areas in southern Belarus and western Russia, was most severely affected by the radioactive fallout, was evacuated between April 1986 and 1995; a total of 170,000 people lost their homes forever and almost everything they owned. The total economic damage caused by the accident is estimated at around 170 billion euros.

The evacuated villagers were settled mainly in villages in the forest steppe of the Kyiv region, where, however, the living conditions were quite different from those in the Polissia water landscape. The citizens of Prypiat were mostly accommodated in newly built districts of Kyiv. The evacuees met with rejection and prejudice from their compatriots, who feared that radioactivity was contagious or were jealous of the priority given to housing. Thousands of pregnant women were urged to have abortions — contraindicated in most cases, as we know today — because of fears that the babies would be deformed. Many evacuees struggled with post-traumatic stress syndrome, experiences of loss, and stress- and radiation-related illnesses. But equally, there was solidarity and self-sacrifice. The "liquidation" of the accident, which involved some 600,000 people from all parts of the Soviet Union, also made Chernobyl a post-Soviet memory site. There is no major city in Russia, Belarus, Ukraine, central Asia, or the Baltic States where Chernobyl liquidators did not live; many cities have Chernobyl memorials.

After the reactor disaster, initially not a Ukrainian but a Soviet history of Chernobyl was written, conveyed with the symbolic language and iconography of the World War experience: the accidental reactor as a war front, the liquidators as heroic partisans and soldiers coming to grips with an invisible enemy.

In this narrative, the role of the villains fell to the power plant personnel, who were blamed for sloppiness and irresponsibility. It was not until years later that an investigative commission pinpointed the main cause of the accident: the accident reactor was defectively designed, but the operating teams at the end of the command lines had been systematically excluded from the flow of information about these defects. These findings, as well as the initial concealment of the extent of the accident, destroyed the confidence of Soviet citizens in the state and nuclear experts. Nevertheless, Chernobyl became the first public catastrophe in Soviet history, of which even pictures were shown, albeit censored ones.

The Ukrainian national history of Chernobyl has often been written with a similar straightforwardness and good/evil distribution. Ambivalences such as the quite successful rooting of Soviet nuclear facilities in the Ukrainian province and the broad participation of Ukrainians in the Soviet nuclear story have not been acknowledged. In this economistic narrative, Ukraine was a passive victim of Moscow technocrats; nuclear power plants were perceived primarily as a Russification agency and a foreign body in their own country. In this reading, the Chernobyl accident was the nail in the coffin of the Soviet Union and the starting point for the Ukrainian independence movement.

But as soon as Ukraine became independent, the Ukrainian elites rediscovered nuclear energy. A nuclear construction moratorium imposed in 1990 was overturned by parliament in 1993. Today, Ukraine has a nuclear power share of about fifty percent, largely based on capacity built after Chernobyl. In the wake of Ukrainian discussions about climate-friendly electricity and energy dependence on Russian gas, Ukrainian nuclear power has been included in the systemically important national infrastructure.

Meanwhile, Chernobyl-Chornobyl is gradually moving from the memory of fellow survivors to the status of a distant historical event and ritualized memorial day. Numerous monuments and a central museum in Kyiv today commemorate the disaster in Ukraine.

In recent years, there have been repeated discussions about whether parts of the exclusion zone could be lifted due to decreasing radioactive contamination, while at the same time, flourishing disaster tourism has developed around the zone. Although the horror of the site is the basis of business for these "Chernobyl Tours," they contribute to its normalization.

Sources

Boltovska, Svetlana: "Local Identities in Ukrainian Polesia and their Transformation under the (Post-)Soviet Nuclear Economy," in *Journal of East Central European Studies* 68 (2019), issue 3, 445-477.

Brown, Kate: *A biography of no place. From ethnic borderland to Soviet heartland*, Cambridge 2004.

Plokhy, Serhii: *Chernobyl: The history of a nuclear catastrophe*, New York 2018.

Wendland, Anna Veronika: "Inventing the Atomograd. Nuclear Urbanism as a Way of Life in Eastern Europe, 1970-2011," in Thomas Bohn, Thomas Feldhoff, Lisette Gebhardt, Arndt Graf (eds.), *The Impact of Disaster: Social and Cultural Approaches to Fukushima and Chernobyl*, 261-287, Berlin 2015.

Wendland, Anna Veronika: "Nuclearizing Ukraine—Ukrainizing the Atom. Soviet nuclear techno-politics, crisis, and resilience at the imperial periphery," in: *Cahiers du Monde Russe* 60 (2019), nos. 2-3, 335-367.

Chernobyl
Disaster without an Aftermath

Rebecca Harms

Two and a half years after the super-GAU [Größter anzuneh-mender Unfall — maximum credible accident] in Unit 4 of the Soviet nuclear power plant Chernobyl, I came to the city of Chornobyl for the first time in October 1988. The Soviet Writers' Union invited other German anti-nuclear activists and me. My last visit to the re-stricted area took place on April 26, 2016, the thirtieth anniversary of the disaster. In April 2021, it will be 35 years of trying to control the consequences of the Unit 4 explosion. Over the decades, mostly returning to the restricted area around anniversaries, I have under-stood that a nuclear catastrophe has no aftermath. For many people of the former Soviet Union, who are now citizens of Ukraine or Bel-arus, the explosion of Unit 4 in Chernobyl destroyed the past and the present. They lost their homes, their graves and their health. The consequences of the biggest nuclear accident so far still affect their children and spoil their future.

When I first came, the Ukrainian journalist and doctor Yuri Shcherbak accompanied me. In his book *Protocols of a Catastrophe*, he describes his days and weeks with the liquidators as a time to look "behind the curtain of night" — "the night that falls when the first nuclear warhead explodes." With him, I looked for the first time at the landscape of Polissia, its abandoned villages, the ghost town of Prypiat and the sarcophagus above unit 4. Yuri Shcherbak brought me to the soldiers, power plant workers, and nuclear work-ers. With him, I approached their dedication, despair, courage, and fatigue. I met Red Army soldiers, firefighters and many others who were declared heroes for their efforts against the radioactive fire and contamination. In the years following the disaster, it became normal to see Chernobyl liquidators as heroes. The Soviet Union had recruited thousands who did not even consider refusing to serve. Most of them suspected more than they knew about what made this mission different from anything they knew.

The road from Kyiv to Chernobyl leads through a rather lonely landscape characterized by forests, fields and small villages. In 1988, the most surprising thing for me was that the road became increasingly crowded the closer we got to the evacuation zone. Full buses shuttled between inside and outside. Trucks carried construction materials and soldiers. Water sprinklers were everywhere on the roads, incessantly washing off the asphalt and impeding traffic. Not outside, but in the restricted area, very large tent camps had been set up, housing only soldiers. The military dominated the scene in the zone. Before the catastrophe, history was divided into the period before and after the "Great Patriotic War". But now we also say, "That was before the war," and mean that was before Chernobyl. Shcherbak described the difficulty of understanding the dangers of the new war. They lurked everywhere, in the balmy wind, in the fragrance of the gardens, in the dust of the roads, in the milk of the cows, and in the fires of leaves and potatoes that had burned everywhere during our journey from Kyiv.

"People are here on a voluntary tour of duty," the head of the information department of the Chernobyl Combine, which had been newly established a few months after the super-GAU, explained to me. Three thousand people worked in the three units of the nuclear power plant. 1500 were involved in decontamination and transport, and about 2000 in supply and infrastructure. In addition, there are always 8000 soldiers in the zone, reservists who have been called up for decontamination work for six months at a time. However, he said the exact scope of the military operation is secret. After the explosion in Block 4, 136,000 people were evacuated from the 30-kilometer zone. In the two and a half years since then, 230,000 civilians had already officially performed cleanup work in that zone. Six hundred thousand people were registered in a Chernobyl medical register and were regularly examined. Visiting the control room of unit 1, we learned that the nuclear center had met the power target in 1988. The three reactors in operation were safe due to technical changes and better training. The world's best robots were being developed for the sarcophagus, which should function even at the highest radiation levels.

Twenty-eight years after this conversation, I came to Chernobyl for the fifth and last time. The Soviet Union had long since ceased to exist. The three reactors that had resumed electricity production a few days after the Super-GAU were no longer running. Unit 2 was shut down in 1991 after a major fire in the turbine hall. The other two were shut down in 1996 and 2000 under pressure from the international community because of serious safety deficiencies. On my last visit, I accompanied a delegation of G7 ambassadors to see the "great arch" that will span and enclose the 1986 sarcophagus. The G7 ambassadors, whose states bore a large part of the cost, were to participate in a commemoration of the victims and heroes of Chernobyl on the occasion of the thirtieth anniversary of the nuclear disaster. And they were to admire the "great arch" together with the president of Ukraine. The work of the builders and the performance of the workers impressed us. We felt tiny under the high shell. The arch had something of a cathedral, some said. A cathedral of the apocalypse said others.

The old sarcophagus, built in 1986 from thousands of tons of steel and tens of thousands of tons of concrete, seemed small, somehow shabby and not so dangerous given the size and perfection of the new shell. As early as 1988, Soviet engineers had declared that the sarcophagus, built very quickly and improvised under the pressure of the catastrophe, would not be able to withstand the loads for a long time. But it was not until 2004 that plans for the new shell became concrete: The arch is 162 meters long and 108 meters high. It weighs 36,000 tons and cost 1.7 billion euros. In November 2016, the news went around the world that the new shell had been successfully pulled over the damaged Block 4 and its sarcophagus on the rails laid for it.

It is tempting to think that the situation is under control 30 years after the disaster. The great arc at Chernobyl provides evidence of just that for supporters of nuclear power. During the thirtieth anniversary visit, in a sober event at the former Chernobyl nuclear power plant, the G7 ambassadors again pledged many hundreds of millions of euros to complete work on the arch and prepare for dismantling the remains of Unit 4. The more speeches I heard about the arch, this cathedral of the apocalypse, the more I understood the message: that humanity can still conquer nuclear fire. Because the controllability of the nuclear catastrophe is suggested, the generosity of some donors is explained.

Based on the book by Nobel Prize winner Svetlana Alexievich, the television series *Chernobyl* has caused a great stir worldwide and in Ukraine. Disaster tourism to the zone, which is strange, is booming. But at a time when many liquidators and contemporary witnesses are already dead, many could recognize what Yuri Shcherbak saw when he looked "behind the curtain of night" in 1986. Or what Alexievich meant when she called her book *A Chronicle of the Future*. If you do not let the "big arch" block your view, you can see three ancient reactors right next door, their fuel rods still stored in pools of water. In the inner zone, there are more than 800 temporary and permanent storage sites for very large quantities of long-lived and hazardous radioactive waste. Almost five percent of Ukraine's territory must be monitored because of soil contamination, including more than 2000 large and small localities. The basin of the Dnipro River, into which the Prypiat flows, must be permanently monitored because the river provides water for 32 million people and irrigation for 1.8 million hectares of land. The health of hundreds of thousands of Ukrainians exposed to acute radiation needs to be monitored regularly. Six million people live in contaminated areas in Ukraine, Belarus and Russia. For a long time since its independence in 1992, Ukraine has had to spend a large part of the state budget on dealing with the consequences of Chernobyl. Shcherbak showed me before and after the collapse of the Soviet Union and before Ukraine's independence that Gorbachev and glasnost failed because of Chernobyl and the corrupt elites of the Soviet nuclear state. We are all still failing because of the catastrophe and the fight against its consequences.

When I returned from my last visit to Chernobyl, I heard a speech by the first president of Ukraine, Leonid Kravchuk. He noted with bitterness that the experience of Chernobyl led Ukrainians to vote in 1992 to give up all nuclear weapons in a referendum he had scheduled. At the time, he said, he thought that was very wise. He had hoped to go down in history as a good president because of it. However, since Russia attacked Ukraine in the east and occupied the Crimean Peninsula, he is ashamed of his misjudgment. Since 2014, the Ukrainian people have again been living in a war they never wanted. However, there is much courage in a new division of time in Ukraine — before and after the Maidan.

Sources

Alexievich, Svetlana: *Chernobyl. A Chronicle of the Future*, Berlin Verlag, Berlin 1997.

Fairlie, Ian: Sumner, David. "The Other Report on Chernobyl (TORCH), Evaluation of Health and Environmental Effects," UK 2006, reprinted 2016.

Harms, Rebecca: "Eine Reise in die Zone," in *the taz*, 15.12.1988, 10-11.

Stscherbak, Jurij: *Protokolle einer Katastrophe*, Athenaeum, Bodenheim 1993.

The Dawn of an Open Society

Eduard Klein

Investigative journalist Mustafa Nayyem certainly had no idea what an avalanche he would unleash. On November 21, 2013, he posted a small message on Facebook calling for a protest rally because Ukrainian President Viktor Yanukovych, under Russian pressure, had not signed the long-negotiated EU Association Agreement at the last moment. A few dozen protesters grew into tens of thousands, then hundreds of thousands until the nationwide protests culminated in the "Revolution of Dignity." This finally put an end to the unpopular, kleptocratic Yanukovych regime.

Disapointed expectations

But as suddenly as this revolutionary moment opened up new perspectives for the country plagued by oligarchy, corruption and mismanagement, this momentum was also massively slowed down again from the outside because only a few days later, the Kremlin tried to prevent the loss of control over Ukraine by military means. And internally, reform-resistant actors in politics and business slammed on the brakes because they wanted to return to the status quo ante. Thus, the country's far-reaching democratic transformation progressed only extremely laboriously and slowly. Two steps forward were usually followed by one step back.

In the meantime, seven years have passed, and the question arises: Where does the country stand today? Many expectations raised by the Maidan were disappointed, first by President Poroshenko, who, as a representative of the old political elite and an oligarch, failed to win over the hearts and minds of Ukrainians. He had to step down in 2019. After Volodymyr Zelenskyy's historic election victory, high hopes rested on Poroshenko's successor. But the political novice also disappointed the people and, after his first year in office, has finally arrived at the troubles of the plain. He is far from fulfilling his two most important promises: He could not end the war in the Donbas, and corruption (especially political corruption) continues unabated. Disappointment is great and is reflected in the polls: Almost three-quarters of respondents to recent polls are dissatisfied with the country's development.

From a closed to an open society

And yet, it must be said: Ukraine *after* the Maidan is a completely different country than Ukraine *before the* Maidan. In recent years, much has been achieved that seemed unthinkable before. Some major reform results are visible and tangible. But most of the changes take place on a small scale in the background and are, therefore, less tangible. Yet they, too, are changing the country step by step.

This became particularly visible in the late summer of 2020, given the events in Belarus. There, the population revolted against the ruler Lukashenka. The autocrat rejected all criticism of the massive electoral fraud, had the peaceful protests brutally suppressed and clung to power.

On the other hand, the change of power in Ukraine in 2019 was peaceful. Open, critical debate is now part of social and political discourse in Ukraine. There is actually an opposition party in parliament, unlike in most post-Soviet states. There is a diverse media landscape (even though many media outlets are in the hands of oligarchs, a certain pluralism results from their rivalry). People in post-Maidan Ukraine are not afraid to express their opinions freely in private conversations or at numerous demonstrations. Ukrainian society is not yet an "open society" in the ideal Popperian sense. But with the Maidan, it has made a great leap toward that goal, away from the post-Soviet, closed society.

Let us just imagine for a moment: What would Ukraine look like today without the Maidan? At that time, Ukraine was at a crossroads. The "dictatorial" tightening of laws passed by Yanukovych on January 16, 2014, to intimidate protesters massively restricted basic democratic rights such as freedom of assembly and expression. Ukraine threatened to follow a similar path to other autocratic states. In Russia, for example, the Kremlin drastically tightened the authoritarian reins after the 2011/12 wave of protests for fear of losing power. This scenario was prevented on the Maidan.

The key to successful reforms

Certainly, a complete reboot of Ukrainian politics has not succeeded even seven years after the Maidan. Oligarchs still control many parties. Deputies use their mandates for informal business instead of representing the interests of their constituents. And neither Poroshenko nor Zelenskyy proved to be the determined corruption fighters they claimed to be. Rather, it is the lively and active civil society that draws attention to problems. It works out solutions and acts as a central corrective when there is once again a threat of backsliding on reforms. The most noticeable progress has been made in areas such as health care, education and public administration, where the interests of the old elites are not so strongly affected. On the other hand, there are still delays in "dicey" issues, such as the fight against political corruption or the urgently needed reform of the judiciary.

But there has also been noticeable progress in some areas previously largely controlled by oligarchies and extremely plagued by corruption, such as the banking and energy sectors. The "sandwich" approach has repeatedly emerged as a model for success: Civil society exerts pressure on decision-makers from within with protests, campaigns and reform proposals. At the same time, the international community uses its financial and diplomatic leverage to exhort the implementation of reforms from the outside. Prime examples of this approach are the independent anti-corruption court, the electronic procurement system Prozorro and the National Anti-Corruption Office. They are considered to be working quite successfully. This approach should therefore be pursued further.

Ukraine needs our support on its rocky road

For Ukrainian society, the Maidan marks the biggest turning point since its independence in 1991. Just as they did on the Maidan, citizens are now defending their newly won freedom in the Donbas —

and paying a high price in blood. As a result, there is no going back to the pre-Maidan era for them. Perhaps this is comparable to the situation in Germany after 1989: Here, too, there was no way for people to return to the old system – despite all the problems that reunification brought with it, some of which still exist today, 30 years later.

We should remember this when we once again receive news about the "chaotic," "corrupt," and simply "unreformable" Ukraine. Because just as people in Leipzig and elsewhere dreamed of freedom and a united Germany in 1989, Ukrainians today dream of a modern, democratic, prosperous, peaceful and eventually reunited state.

Ukraine itself must tread this long and rocky path. The Maidan was certainly not the end. Rather, it was the signal of departure that set the direction of travel for the country in the direction of Europe. Germany and Europe should therefore stand up for their European values and, not least out of their own interests, end the war on their own doorstep. We should accompany Ukraine and its committed citizens on their difficult path with empathy, support and determination.

The text is based on an article by the author in Ukraine-Analyses and has been extensively revised for this publication.

Medusa and the Jellyfish Museum

Kateryna Mishchenko

For the past several years, I have tried to avoid Independence Square. It is not because of the sorrow that is felt there today but because there is not much space left for this sorrow or the experience of the winter of 2014. A strange life of normality has returned with its animated animals, the throng of children in the summer as they splash in the fountains, electric scooters, friends meeting, and invitations to go on excursions to Mezhyhirya Park. Here you can have a picture taken with a tired eagle or an owl. The owl looks around as if to wonder why the girls take such attractive selfies against the background of just anything. Even bouquets of flowers and photographs of the deceased are along the pavement of Insty-tutska Street. I am not actually sure, however, that this everyday life is not just a layer of soft powder meant to conceal wounds.

I recently visited the Maidan, starting with the underground Globe Shopping Center, frozen in time from the protests. It withstood even the worst of times and then carried out repairs, although the air still retains a sinister and persistent silence. This leaves a feeling more unpleasant than any other shopping mall you might visit. One of the floors in the Globe takes you straight to the ceiling space. There is also an air of something both taciturn and still—a clear sense of unutterable forced silence. It is strange how this small piece of Maidan square can exist in its own sound mode. The paving stones here are old and cracked, some are completely missing, but they are a rare, unmasked vestige of the events of that time. The place is like an abandoned amphitheater, with its high steps arranged in a semicircle steeped in alcohol. There are often groups of teenagers sitting around here, but no matter how much fun they are having, they are still not loud.

The recreational area appears to be spontaneously diminishing. The monument remains a gathering place for various political rallies. There is an outdoor exhibition of the still unbuilt Museum of the Revolution of Dignity with large information placards about the various aspects of the 2013–2014 protests. Such is the mark of time on the Maidan: people sitting around on the lawns, resting in the present day, and here in the middle of silence, the future and the past are intertwined in a bundle of nerves that periodically generates anxiety.

Mirage

One September Saturday, a group of Ukrainian and Belarusian activists gathered near the monument; some of them had just recently arrived from Belarus. Their words were filled with passion and hope. This passion has to be supported. That day, their action focused on solidarity with women and their special role in protests. The demonstration moves from the Maidan to the Embassy of Belarus. I notice the queue at Zara in Khreshchatyk; the number of people is about the same as today's line of demonstrators. The passersby encourage the column, and cars beep their horns. The city understands well what is happening and how high the stakes are. Kyiv is striving for "normality" while at the same time supporting the Belarusians.

The current events in the neighboring country make us think back to how we felt during the already-forgotten events of the winter of 2014 and ask ourselves what exactly we should have done differently. A filter comes down, and through it, you suddenly see new facets of your own nostalgia. I like the absence of the far-right, the explicit non-violence of the citizens, and the feminist iconography of the Belarusian summer. The rays of the summer sun illuminate an image of the Maidan—a twilight winter settlement with its short days and long restless nights. A sense of the fatality of everything that happens when there is nowhere to hide from the cynical violence of power. Then there are still those unresolved questions I do not know where to address: to the past or the future. What does it mean to fight back in the conditions of such a regime? What does it mean to do everything you can to avoid being accused of provoking foreign military intervention, although you are simply defending your basic civil rights? What is left of you when you are being bullied into thinking about images of the Second World War? Will you go out onto the street again? How can you treat agoraphobia if there was no rule of law and there still is not?

Revolutionary moments are staged in different ways. It is interesting how they stimulate each other's reinterpretation and the form in which they enter into dialogue. The Maidan seems to be a lesson learned. It was said that there was a lot of geopolitics and violence on the part of the protesters, as well as an anti-Russian position that provoked Russia's military intervention. Sometimes from the distance of time, it is difficult to assess the real anti-violence intention which brought hundreds of thousands of people out into the streets. From the distance of time, even if you look closely, the Maidan today has become a hostage of official nationalist discourse, acquiring the name "Revolution of Dignity". The violence of the hardline power structures and the absolute vulnerability of citizens are now a discursive shadow. Therefore, those who have experience of the Maidan, rather than those who created its image post factum, are the first to recognize the despair of the Belarusians and the risks they are taking.

In addition to bloodless success, my hopes for Belarusian protests are that they will give us Ukrainians and the societies in neighboring countries a new aesthetics of protests: strikes, decentralization, and an emphasis on rights, rather than national identity. In this aesthetic, there will no longer be a place for the old-school discourses of farewell to the Soviet empire. It will be formed by conscious social vulnerability, the solidarity of professional communities, sensitivity to the emancipatory currents of recent decades, and the desire for democratic interaction.

Can a new quality of civil discord be formed against a background of the hegemony born of the bellicose spirit of paramilitary groups and fashion for right-wing aesthetics? The events of Belorussia give me such hope. Their restlessness and fluidity can irrigate dry lands and create oases of a new sociality. No one can guarantee continued existence, and at this time, the precious nature of their lives becomes even more obvious.

Medusa and the Jellyfish Museum

I turn back from the experience of life to the dystopian memorial landscape around the Maidan monument. The information on the placards I have already referred to is built on the principle of comparing the events, protagonists or episodes of the Maidan with analogies from the liberation history of Ukraine. Many analogies have been drawn with the Ukrainian Sich Riflemen — a national military formation that fought against the Russian Empire as part of the Austro-Hungarian armed forces. The as-yet-unbuilt Museum of the Revolution of Dignity thus tells the story of the Sich riflemen and introduces its conceptual approach, but what do we learn about the Maidan? What is its role — is it the consolidation of the timeless myth of the liberation struggle? Are the Maidan participants, including the Heavenly Hundred Heroes, primarily romantic freedom fighters?

Quite demonstratively, the territory where the museum was to be built has been cordoned off by the Prosecutor General's Office. This is due to the need to conduct investigative experiments related to the shootings on Instytutska Street. While the museum is not physically present, we can still admire its foundations. We can still appreciate the long-standing and long-suffering investigations, the desires of the loved ones of those who died on the Maidan and human rights activists to preserve Instytutska Street in its current form because, in fact, it is the only testimony to real events, as well as the spontaneous memorial sites which are still being cared for.

While Instytutska Street lives on as a disputed territory, at the very end of the street, at the intersection with Khreshchatyk, there is a private Museum of Jellyfish. If you look up from Instytutska Street, its enormous blue signboard is a huge eye-catcher. One day I went there with my little son. It is a small place with a number of different rooms with aquariums lit in different colors where the most diverse range of jellyfish swim around. You can see how the newly born creatures of this beautiful species turn into adults. It is just a short walk. As we leave the museum, my son bashes his forehead against the glass wall, cries and continues to weep outside at the bottom of Instytutska Street.

The figure of Medusa has a rich history. The image of her severed head was affixed to combat shields to scare the enemy away and burial plates to protect graves from being plundered. In this way, the Kyiv urban unconscious offers its own version of the memorialization of the Maidan experience. In the embers of the revolution, a museum has emerged, which we currently deserve.

September 2020

A Successful Decommunization?

Sébastien Gobert

On a shield of 13 by 8 meters, a hammer and a sickle are intertwined. From the top of its 62 meters, the monumental "Motherland" contemplates Kyiv and Ukraine beyond. Since the entry by force of the four so-called decommunization laws[1] on May 21, 2015, the statue has witnessed the renaming of almost 52,000 streets across the country, more than 1,000 localities, 26 raions (districts), and 30 ports and railway stations. Even 70 towns in the annexed Crimea were renamed as wishful thinking on the proposal of the Tatar Mejlis. Two thousand five hundred monuments, including 1300 statues of Lenin, have disappeared from the Ukrainian public space in an unprecedented movement of "Leninopad" (literally translated as "Lenin's fall")[2]. But the Motherland remains unperturbed, unaltered for technical reasons. At the time of writing, in September 2020, it is still the symbol of an unfinished decommunization.

It is unfinished, first of all, concerning the facts. If the former director of the Institute of National Memory Volodymyr Vyatrovich had assured that Ukraine was "Lenin-free" by the end of 2016, his successor Anton Drobovych revealed, in September 2020, that dozens of statues are intact "in inconspicuous places", as well as thousands of communist symbols. The hammer, sickle and five-pointed star are, in fact, exhibited even in the center of Kyiv, despite

---

1   One law "condemns the communist and nazi totalitarian regimes" and prohibits the promotion of their symbols. A second gives official status to "fighters for Ukrainian independence in the 20th century". A third defines the memory of "the victory over Nazism during the Second World War" (as opposed to the Soviet designation of the Great Patriotic War, ed. note). Finally, a fourth one orders the opening of the archives of the "repressive organs" of the period 1917-91.

2   These statistics do not include the changes that occurred between the start of Leninopad in November 2013 and the entry into force of the laws. Therefore, the number of Lenin statues that have been toppled or debunked since 2013 is larger, estimated to be more than 2000.

a legal prohibition. While many observers refer to Ukraine to try to explain the debunking and attacks on historical statues around the world, the question of the success of Ukrainian de-communization is very relative and necessarily subjective.

Differentiated acceptances and attempts to backtrack

In the minds of Ukrainians, de-communization does not seem to have a consensus. A survey conducted by the Democratic Initiatives Fund in April 2020 reveals that the removal of monuments and symbols of the communist era is disapproved by 34% of the respondents; 32% support it, and 26.3% are indifferent. Thirty-four percent agree with the decision to designate the USSR as a "totalitarian state that practiced terror", 31.3% disagree, and 15.4% are indifferent. As for the changes in the names of streets and cities, the division is clearer: 44% against, 29.9% for and 19.9% neutral. The survey also confirms the observations made in *Looking for Lenin*: the positions of Ukrainians are formed by generational and geographical factors, but also social, political and environmental (in the sociological sense of the term).

This division of public opinion on the appreciation of the fait accompli of decommunization is accentuated by pronounced resistance. In February 2020, the Kharkiv City Council reversed a 2016 decision by renaming Petro Hrihorenko Avenue in honor of Soviet Marshal Zhukov. For the mayor, Hennadiy Kernes, it was a matter of "defending the historical memory." A group of national deputies had also tried to invalidate the law prohibiting "the promotion of symbols of totalitarian communist or Nazi regimes" before being rejected by the constitutional court in 2019. The slogans accompanying the occasional criminal sanctions against citizens displaying communist symbols still demonstrate the reluctance of a part of the population to comply with the de-communization laws.

Between approval and opposition, it is also worth mentioning the fatigue of Ukrainians regarding the memorial debates. If it is perceptible in the above-mentioned survey, it was clearly expressed in April 2019 by the election of Volodymyr Zelenskyy as president at the expense of Petro Poroshenko. The latter had openly engraved the memorial issues in his election campaign. On the other hand, his successor has distanced himself from historical controversies. This discontinuity in state policy, visibly appreciated by a significant part of the population, calls into question the very coherence of the decommunization enterprise.

Undeniable lessons from Ukrainian-style decommunization

Divided as to the outcome of its own Leninopad, Ukraine cannot claim to be a model for other countries where statues of slavers or dictators fall. Nevertheless, a number of lessons can be drawn from it, starting with the similarities of the scenes of unbolting or falling. The attack on a statue of Lenin was not so much aimed at the historical personality of the Bolshevik leader as at the ideas and political system he represented. In Ukraine, as elsewhere, the revolutionary act of tearing down a statue, in the sense of tearing down an ideology, cannot be underestimated.

From this perspective, de-communization has achieved undeniable objectives, even if they are difficult to quantify. On the one hand, it acts as a physical marker of identity vis-à-vis the temporarily occupied territories of Crimea, Donetsk, and Luhansk, where statues of Lenin are preserved and restored. The 2015 laws also established a clear distancing from Soviet and Russian historiography, especially in the treatment of World War II. The opening of archives plays a crucial role in this, both for historians and for the families of victims of repression. In the long term, de-communization can change the citizens' approach to history by making it more accessible. It has also been part of the structural process of decentralization, encouraging thousands of localities to devise new place names.

Decommunization, and after?

On the other hand, it is clear that five years of de-communization have not allowed the emergence of a consensual discourse on the upheavals of the twentieth century and the Soviet past. Volodymyr Vyatrovich's repeated calls for a "decolonization" of Ukraine have hardly been echoed in society. The definition of a balanced historiography on the shortcomings and benefits of 70 years of Soviet rule is still struggling. Some point to the speed and radicalness of the Leninopad and the implementation of the laws to explain the current resistance. The geopolitical context, as well as the extreme politicization of certain categories of society and the difficulty of structuring a constructive debate, seem nevertheless to be better indicators. The controversies and polemics, both on issues related to de-communization and on the subjects of Babi Yar, the Holodomor or Ukrainian-Polish relations, attest to the fact that memory issues are often held hostage to current events.

Through the lack of historiographical consensus within Ukrainian society, it is the lack of a common vision for the future that shines through. It concerns both the definition of the protection of the Ukrainian artistic heritage and the preservation of communist monuments, and the erection of new national heroes to replace the Soviet icons. Volodymyr Vyatrovich's focus on controversial nationalist figures has contributed greatly to exacerbating antagonistic positions.

Finally, de-communization must be understood in the unique context of the Revolution of Dignity, the annexation of Crimea and the war in Donbas. According to a study by the Fund for Democratic Initiatives, 68% of those who support the disappearance of communist symbols want European integration of Ukraine. However, obstacles have accumulated on the road to reform, political renewal and improvement of living standards. However, it is a profound transformation of Ukraine that will consecrate a real break with the Soviet past, much more than removing a hammer and a sickle from the shield of the Motherland.

"To succeed Ukraine needs more trust and strong institutions" — if one was looking for a generalization of 30 years of Western advice to Ukraine, this would be it. Afterall, trust and strength of system of rules are the very cornerstones of the success of the European and North American societies. Even further, no Asian transformation in the XX century was successful without the same ingredients. Ukraine ranks below top-100 countries in most rankings that measure quality of institutions, it sits around #100 in infrastructure rankings, and significantly higher, sometimes even within top 50 on human capital rankings. Ronald Inglehart's World Values Survey puts Ukraine above the USA, Belgium or Poland measuring secular-rational vs traditional values. Why then Ukrainians do not follow the beneficial principles that it is better to trust than not, it is better to follow the rules than not? Why do they cling to a corrupt system and have their governance backwards?

The answer is a logical one. And it comes from impressive representative sample of tens of millions of cases, spread over the last century, still alive in the living memory of a very diverse nation.

Two major traumas define the Ukrainian history of the XX century: the trauma of totalitarianism, and the colonial trauma. While many countries of the world have suffered from strong and abusive governments and a colonial rule, it is a particular way how the two are combined in the case of Ukraine that they produce a perfect storm.

The Ukrainian experience with totalitarianism is often reduced to the period of Stalin. It is true that after Stalin the USSR never returned to the very same practices of exterminating millions of people. Stalin left a legacy, still visible through the Ukrainian demography—the extermination of the entire strata of successful farmers and their economic, social and religious connections, the catastrophic experiences of the WWII, which had its cruelest and bloodies events taking place in Ukraine are felt even generations after. Ukraine eventually had not managed to restore its demographic trends in the XX century, now demographic decline is, probably, its gravest strategic challenge.

The Khrushchev thaw and Briezhniev era, however backward and still repressive, were much closer to autocracy than totalitarian regime. What it often overlooked is that if fascist Italy or nazi Germany totalitarianism gave way to restoring democracy, in the USSR the fear of return to Stalinist practices was never off the agenda. The wounds went deep as people of the European breadbasket were forced to resort to cannibalism to survive with Holodomor taking over 3 million lives in conservative estimates. The survivors had a chance of being tortured to death as part of the Nazi collective responsibility practices for the offences they never did, and the survivors taken to Siberia only for the sole fact that they resided on the occupied territory — the WWII had also a toll of millions of Ukrainian lives.

The dissident movement tensed the Soviet regime, to govern in Ukraine in much rougher terms than in Russia or other parts of the USSR. And when with the beginning of Perestroika it almost seemed like the bad luck was over and the scary pages of history can be turned, Chornobyl nuclear disaster happened just outside of Kyiv, and the Communist party decided to show the business-as-usual approach by forcing the school children to participate in a May Day parade under radioactive clouds.

The untreated totalitarian trauma would be reactivated with every recurring oppressive action or a catastrophe, exacerbated by bad or malice governance. Since the trauma itself was never identified and healed, it stored itself in the culture, sending a vivid message to the citizens: no one has killed or endangered more people in the history of Ukraine than a ruling government, the government is people's greatest threat. And, since the government cannot be contained or made accountable, it is safest for the people if the government is weak and incapable [of harming people]. The discourse of the very same trauma views corruption as the tool of last resort, placing it into the category of instruments for survival, not the burden of inefficiency. Inefficiency [of the government] means greater safety [for the people].

The very collapse of the Soviet Union was a stark reminder that things may turn worse, when a group of hardliners staged a coup in Moscow and threatened to renew Stalinist practices. Millions of Ukrainians, who had just supported the idea of a renewed Soviet Union on a referendum March 17, 1991 (70% in favor, 84% voter turnout) turned around at instant overwhelmingly opposing it and backing independence instead December 1, 1991 (90% in favor, 84% voter turnout). Historians still debate whether the Soviet system indeed had the capacity to turn back to old practices, but the Ukrainian society wanted to take no chances.

However scared of Soviet repressions the society was, on the same date it supported the independence, it has clearly given a landslide victory to a communist president. The people delegated the authorities the mandate to change anything necessary so as little as possible would be actually changed.

Their next choice of leadership in 1994 was a different representative of the same communist elite. It was only in 2014 that Ukrainians entrusted the most powerful post in the government to a person, who has never been a communist party member, though rather because of age, not the family background. And it was only after Euromaidan of 2014 that Ukraine has finally detached itself from the Soviet legacy, opening the doors to reshaping the governance model to a friendlier government that serves the people. By this time the society has adapted its skill to weaken the government by not providing it with institutional trust. While church, civil society and volunteer networks enjoyed institutional trust in the range of 50-70%, the parliament, the cabinet, the courts hardly rose above 25%, sometimes dipping into singe-digit numbers, with local self-governance performing only slightly better. Trust is the scarcest of the resources in Ukraine. With Ukraine's history it is understandable: the ones who trusted, usually were the first to lose their lives.

The healing could come from developing a model, which would acknowledge the unique cultural circumstances, allow the citizens to have control over the government through greater accountability as well as checks and balances system.

Ukraine has been part of three very different institutional traditions — its parts were in Russian, Austrian-Hungarian, and Ottoman empires, its mainstream belongs to Orthodox, Catholic Christian and Sunni Muslim religions with multiple denominations, its ethnic identity is predominantly Ukrainian.

but Ukraine is also home to Crimean Tatars, it used to have a large Jewish community, and there are many minority groups which add to the diversity of Ukraine. The Ukrainian governance model would have to adapt to this diversity, stretching beyond the usual European parameters of a nation-state based on mature identity. Ukraine definitely falls into a category of a nation-state, but too many of its future institutions are still stem-cells today, allowing for a more efficient and modern design, but lacking the clear model to build around.

Arriving to such model would require Ukraine to have its own schools of thought and capacity to theorize in security, law, justice, representation, economic, social issues. But this is where the other trauma comes in: the Ukrainian cultural identity after being conquered by the Russian Czars late XVIII century, has kept its candle burning for generations, but went mainstream only recently, gaining access to managerial and governing positions for the first time in, probably, a dozen generations. As the Soviet and Russian governance legacy stayed predominantly in Russian cultural domain, Ukrainians found themselves making governance model decisions, while hardly being equipped with knowledge, experience and good advice.

"To succeed Ukraine needs more trust and strong institutions" mantra comes on top of the hardly treated trauma, but into a rapidly developing environment where more and more young and exposed to the outside world people become capable of taking responsibility and assuming leadership on many levels.

To overcome generations of fear, bad memories they need the basics that any of the developed countries had in the beginning of modern transformation—the capacity to provide one's own security. That same capacity which the European Union members and Asian tigers alike only partially provided themselves, but mostly received as an external assistance from the Americans.

Given greater security, Ukraine with its passionate domestic civil society actors and promising young political scene, would be able to do the rest of its homework on its own, providing the ray of hope for Russia and other former Soviet countries.

Unless the West fails Ukraine with another set of well-intended, but unhelpful advice.

The Ukrainian Trauma

Yevhen Hlibovytsky

"To succeed Ukraine needs more trust and strong institutions" — if one was looking for a generalization of 30 years of Western advice to Ukraine, this would be it. Afterall, trust and strength of system of rules are the very cornerstones of the success of the European and North American societies. Even further, no Asian transformation in the XX century was successful without the same ingredients. Ukraine ranks below top-100 countries in most rankings that measure quality of institutions, it sits around #100 in infrastructure rankings, and significantly higher, sometimes even within top 50 on human capital rankings. Ronald Inglehart's World Values Survey puts Ukraine above the USA, Belgium or Poland measuring secular-rational vs traditional values. Why then Ukrainians do not follow the beneficial principles that it is better to trust than not, it is better to follow the rules than not? Why do they cling to a corrupt system and have their governance backwards?

The answer is a logical one. And it comes from impressive representative sample of tens of millions of cases, spread over the last century, still alive in the living memory of a very diverse nation.

Two major traumas define the Ukrainian history of the XX century: the trauma of totalitarianism, and the colonial trauma. While many countries of the world have suffered from strong and abusive governments and a colonial rule, it is a particular way how the two are combined in the case of Ukraine that they produce a perfect storm.

The Ukrainian experience with totalitarianism is often reduced to the period of Stalin. It is true that after Stalin the USSR never returned to the very same practices of exterminating millions of people. Stalin left a legacy, still visible through the Ukrainian demography — the extermination of the entire strata of successful farmers and their economic, social and religious connections, the catastrophic experiences of the WWII, which had its cruelest and bloodies events taking place in Ukraine are felt even generations after. Ukraine eventually had not managed to restore its demographic trends in the XX century, now demographic decline is, probably, its gravest strategic challenge.

The Khrushchev thaw and Briezhniev era, however backward and still repressive, were much closer to autocracy than totalitarian regime. What it often overlooked is that if fascist Italy or nazi Germany totalitarianism gave way to restoring democracy, in the USSR the fear of return to Stalinist practices was never off the agenda. The wounds went deep as people of the European breadbasket were forced to resort to cannibalism to survive with Holodomor taking over 3 million lives in conservative estimates. The survivors had a chance of being tortured to death as part of the Nazi collective responsibility practices for the offences they never did, and the survivors taken to Siberia only for the sole fact that they resided on the occupied territory — the WWII had also a toll of millions of Ukrainian lives.

The dissident movement tensed the Soviet regime, to govern in Ukraine in much rougher terms than in Russia or other parts of the USSR. And when with the beginning of Perestroika it almost seemed like the bad luck was over and the scary pages of history can be turned, Chornobyl nuclear disaster happened just outside of Kyiv, and the Communist party decided to show the business-as-usual approach by forcing the school children to participate in a May Day parade under radioactive clouds.

The untreated totalitarian trauma would be reactivated with every recurring oppressive action or a catastrophe, exacerbated by bad or malice governance. Since the trauma itself was never identified and healed, it stored itself in the culture, sending a vivid message to the citizens: no one has killed or endangered more people in the history of Ukraine than a ruling government, the government is people's greatest threat. And, since the government cannot be contained or made accountable, it is safest for the people if the government is weak and incapable [of harming people]. The discourse of the very same trauma views corruption as the tool of last resort, placing it into the category of instruments for survival, not the burden of inefficiency. Inefficiency [of the government] means greater safety [for the people].

The very collapse of the Soviet Union was a stark reminder that things may turn worse, when a group of hardliners staged a coup in Moscow and threatened to renew Stalinist practices. Millions of Ukrainians, who had just supported the idea of a renewed Soviet Union on a referendum March 17, 1991 (70% in favor, 84% voter turnout) turned around at instant overwhelmingly opposing it and backing independence instead December 1, 1991 (90% in favor, 84% voter turnout). Historians still debate whether the Soviet system indeed had the capacity to turn back to old practices, but the Ukrainian society wanted to take no chances.

However scared of Soviet repressions the society was, on the same date it supported the independence, it has clearly given a landslide victory to a communist president. The people delegated the authorities the mandate to change anything necessary so as little as possible would be actually changed.

Their next choice of leadership in 1994 was a different representative of the same communist elite. It was only in 2014 that Ukrainians entrusted the most powerful post in the government to a person, who has never been a communist party member, though rather because of age, not the family background. And it was only after Euromaidan of 2014 that Ukraine has finally detached itself from the Soviet legacy, opening the doors to reshaping the governance model to a friendlier government that serves the people. By this time the society has adapted its skill to weaken the government by not providing it with institutional trust. While church, civil society and volunteer networks enjoyed institutional trust in the range of 50-70%, the parliament, the cabinet, the courts hardly rose above 25%, sometimes dipping into singe-digit numbers, with local self-governance performing only slightly better. Trust is the scarcest of the resources in Ukraine. With Ukraine's history it is understandable: the ones who trusted, usually were the first to lose their lives.

The healing could come from developing a model, which would acknowledge the unique cultural circumstances, allow the citizens to have control over the government through greater accountability as well as checks and balances system.

Ukraine has been part of three very different institutional traditions — its parts were in Russian, Austrian-Hungarian, and Ottoman empires, its mainstream belongs to Orthodox, Catholic Christian and Sunni Muslim religions with multiple denominations, its ethnic identity is predominantly Ukrainian.

but Ukraine is also home to Crimean Tatars, it used to have a large Jewish community, and there are many minority groups which add to the diversity of Ukraine. The Ukrainian governance model would have to adapt to this diversity, stretching beyond the usual European parameters of a nation-state based on mature identity. Ukraine definitely falls into a category of a nation-state, but too many of its future institutions are still stem-cells today, allowing for a more efficient and modern design, but lacking the clear model to build around.

Arriving to such model would require Ukraine to have its own schools of thought and capacity to theorize in security, law, justice, representation, economic, social issues. But this is where the other trauma comes in: the Ukrainian cultural identity after being conquered by the Russian Czars late XVIII century, has kept its candle burning for generations, but went mainstream only recently, gaining access to managerial and governing positions for the first time in, probably, a dozen generations. As the Soviet and Russian governance legacy stayed predominantly in Russian cultural domain, Ukrainians found themselves making governance model decisions, while hardly being equipped with knowledge, experience and good advice.

"To succeed Ukraine needs more trust and strong institutions" mantra comes on top of the hardly treated trauma, but into a rapidly developing environment where more and more young and exposed to the outside world people become capable of taking responsibility and assuming leadership on many levels.

To overcome generations of fear, bad memories they need the basics that any of the developed countries had in the beginning of modern transformation — the capacity to provide one's own security. That same capacity which the European Union members and Asian tigers alike only partially provided themselves, but mostly received as an external assistance from the Americans.

Given greater security, Ukraine with its passionate domestic civil society actors and promising young political scene, would be able to do the rest of its homework on its own, providing the ray of hope for Russia and other former Soviet countries.

Unless the West fails Ukraine with another set of well-intended, but unhelpful advice.

About the Authors

Applebaum, Anne (* 1964), journalist and historian specializing in Central and Eastern Europe. She writes for *The Atlantic*, formerly for The *Washington Post*, and is a senior fellow at Johns Hopkins University. She won the Pulitzer Prize for her book *Gulag: A History* (2004) and has written: *Red Famine* (2017) and *Twilight of Democracy: The Seductive Lure of Authoritarianism* (2019), among others.

Beck, Marieluise (* 1952) was a member of the German Bundestag from 1983 to 2017 and State Secretary at the Federal Ministry of Family Affairs, Senior Citizens, Women and Youth from 2002 to 2005. In 2017, she co-founded the Center for Liberal Modernity (LibMod) in Berlin.

Behrends, Dr. Jan Claas (* 1969), Eastern European historian specializing in the contemporary history of Eastern Europe, urban history, European dictatorships, and research on violence, and project director at the Center for Contemporary History, Potsdam. His publications include *The Invented Friendship. Propaganda for the Soviet Union in Poland and in the GDR* (2006) and numerous articles in scientific journals.

Berkhoff, Dr. Karel C. (* 1965), Eastern European historian specializing in Ukraine and the Holocaust. He researches Babyn Yar at the *NIOD Institute for War, Holocaust and Genocide Studies*, Amsterdam. His publications include *Harvest of Despair: Life and Death in Ukraine Under Nazi Rule* (2004) and *Motherland in Danger: Soviet Propaganda During World War II* (2012).

Brumme, Christoph (* 1962), essayist and writer, writes novels and reportages about his bicycle journeys from Berlin to the Volga and back, among other things. His publications include *111 Reasons to Love Ukraine*. He has lived in the eastern Ukrainian city of Poltava since the spring of 2016.

Christ, Sebastian (* 1981), author, journalist and futurologist. He has been the editor for digital policy at *Der Tagesspiegel* since 2018. Previously, he worked as a freelance journalist in Kyiv. As an author, he published, among others: *The Growl of Tanks in Spring. A War Report from Afghanistan* (2011) and *My False Brothers: How I Joined the Islamic State as a 16-Year-Old* (2017).

Gobert, Sébastien (* 1985), a freelance journalist based in Kyiv since 2011, reports for *Libération*, *Radio France Internationale*, *Le Monde Diplomatique* and *La Tribune de Genève*, among others. Founder of the collective "Daleko-Blisko", co-author of *Looking for Lenin* with Niels Ackermann (FUEL editions, 2017).

Grinchenko, Prof. Dr. Gelinada (* 1971), professor of history at the Faculty of Ukrainian Studies (Faculty of Philosophy, National V.-N. Karazin University, Kharkiv, Ukraine), Editor-in-Chief of the academic journal *Ukraina Moderna*, Head of the *Ukrainian Oral History Society* and member of the German-Ukrainian Historians' Commission (DUHK).

Grytsenko, Oksana (* 1981), freelance journalist based in Kyiv. She worked for the *Kyiv Post* for nine years. She publishes in the *Guardian*, *AFP* and other international media. She also writes plays and screenplays.

Harms, Rebecca (* 1956), co-founder of the anti-nuclear movement in Germany. Green politician, member of the European Parliament 2004–2019. Her focus is on environmental, climate and energy policy and Eastern Europe.

Hlibovytsky, Yevhen (* 1975), founder of the pro.mova think tank, which studies the impact of culture on institutional development. He is a member of the Nestor Group, where experts from various fields and institutions discuss Ukraine's development, and he is a lecturer at the Ukrainian Catholic University in Lviv.

Jilge, Wilfried (* 1970) is a historian of Eastern Europe focusing on the contemporary history and politics of Ukraine and Russia. He is an associate fellow of the *German Council on Foreign Relations (DGAP)* in Berlin and a permanent member of the Strategy Group "Key States" in the Bertelsmann Stiftung's "Strategies for the EU Neighborhood" project.

Klein, Dr. Eduard (* 1982), research associate at the *Research Center for Eastern Europe at the* University of Bremen and editor of *Ukraine-Analysen*. He received his doctorate on corruption in Ukrainian and Russian higher education and previously worked, among other things, as an editor at *dekoder*, as a research assistant in the German Bundestag and as a consultant at the Center for Liberal Modernity.

Klimeniouk, Nikolai (* 1970), freelance writer and project manager at the European Exchange for *Quorum initiative*. As an author, he writes regularly for the *Frankfurter Allgemeine Sonntagszeitung, Neue Zürcher Zeitung* and other German and European media.

Kuleba, Dmytro (* 1981) is Minister of Foreign Affairs and a member of the National Defense and Security Council of Ukraine. Kuleba has served in Ukraine's diplomatic service since 2003, and became the youngest foreign affairs minister in Ukraine's history in 2020. He worked as Deputy Prime Minister of Ukraine for European and Euro-Atlantic Integration in 2019-2020, and Permanent Representative of Ukraine to the Council of Europe in 2016-2019.

Mishchenko, Kateryna (* 1984), author, translator and publisher. She is the co-founder and editor of the Ukrainian publishing house Medusa and co-author of the book Ukrainian Night (together with Miron Zownir). Her essays have appeared in international journals and anthologies about the Maidan, published by Suhrkamp.

Plokhy, Prof. Dr. Serhii (* 1957), Eastern European historian specializing in Ukraine, and director of the Harvard Ukrainian Research Institute. His publications include *The Cossack Myth: History* *and Nationhood in the Age of Empires* (2012), *The Gates of Europe: A History of Ukraine* (2015), and *Chernobyl: History of a Tragedy* (2018).

Savchuk, Viktoria (* 1992), lawyer and activist. She is a co-editor at the *Berlin Info-Point Crimea* initiative and worked at the NGO *Crimea SOS*. Since 2019 she has been working at the Center for Liberal Modernity.

Sherbakova, Dr. Irina (* 1949), Germanist and historian specializing in oral history, totalitarianism, Stalinism, Gulag and Soviet special camps on German soil after 1945. She deals with questions of cultural memory in Russia and the politics of remembrance. She is a founding member of *Memorial* and the author of numerous books, including *Der Russland-Reflex* (2015) with Karl Schlögel.

Simon, Prof. em. Dr. Gerhard (* 1937), historian and Slavist specializing in Russia and the other states of the CIS. He was a research associate at the Federal Institute for East European and International Studies in Cologne and a professor of history at the University of Cologne. He is currently working on authoritarian regimes, democratization in the CIS region, and current developments in Ukraine and Russia.

Snyder, Prof. Dr. Timothy (* 1969), a historian specializing in Eastern Europe and the Holocaust. He is a professor at Yale University and a permanent fellow at the *Vienna Institute for Human Sciences*. As an author, he has published numerous books, including *Bloodlands* (2010) and *On Tyranny* (2017).

Traşcă, Dr. Ottmar (* 1969), a historian specializing in Romania during World War II. He earned his doctorate in Romanian-German political-military relations from 1940–1944. As a fellow of the Alexander von Humboldt Foundation, he is researching "Intelligence with the Ally: Abwehrstelle Rumänien—ihre Partner, Konkurrenten und Gegner 1940-1944."

Von Twickel, Nikolaus (* 1969), editor of the website *Understanding Russia* at the Center for Liberal Modernity. As a journalist, he worked at the *Moscow Times* and, among others, at the *Deutsche Presse-Agentur*. In 2015/16, he was a media liaison officer for the OSCE Observer Mission in Donetsk, Ukraine. Among other things, he writes a newsletter for *DRA e. V.* about the situation in the eastern Ukrainian "People's Republics". Together with Thomas de Waal, he published the book *Beyond Frozen Conflict* (2020).

Wendland, Dr. Anna Veronika (* 1966), historian of Eastern Europe and technology, research coordinator in the directorate of the Marburg Herder Institute for Historical Research on Eastern Central Europe and project manager in the Collaborative Research Center SFB Transregio 138 "Dynamics of Security". She is also a member of the Petersburg Dialogue and the German-Ukrainian Historical Commission (DUHK).

Wolschner, Klaus (* 1951), was editor of the *taz* from 1979 to 2013 and has been a lecturer in cultural and media studies at the University of Bremen since 2005.

Yermolenko, Dr. Volodymyr (* 1980), philosopher, essayist, editor-in-chief of the online platform *UkraineWorld* and head of the political analysis department at *Internews Ukraine*. In 2019, he edited the anthology *Ukraine in Histories and Stories: Essays by Ukrainian Intellectuals*. He also teaches at the Kyiv Mohlya Academy and is a member of *PEN Ukraine*.

UKRAINIAN VOICES

Collected by Andreas Umland

Sergiy Korsunsky, Kobe Gakuin University, Japan

Nadiia Koval, Kyiv School of Economics, Ukraine

Volodymyr Kravchenko, University of Alberta, Edmonton

Oleksiy Kresin, NAS Koretskiy Institute of State and Law, Kyiv

Anatoliy Kruglashov, Fedkovych National University, Chernivtsi

Andrey Kurkov, PEN Ukraine, Kyiv

Ostap Kushnir, Lazarski University, Warsaw

Taras Kuzio, National University of Kyiv-Mohyla Academy

Serhii Kvit, National University of Kyiv-Mohyla Academy

Yuliya Ladygina, The Pennsylvania State University, USA

Yevhen Mahda, Institute of World Policy, Kyiv

Victoria Malko, California State University, Fresno, USA

Yulia Marushevska, Security and Defense Center (SAND), Kyiv

Myroslav Marynovych, Ukrainian Catholic University, Lviv

Oleksandra Matviichuk, Center for Civil Liberties, Kyiv

Mykhailo Minakov, Kennan Institute, Washington, USA

Anton Moiseienko, The Australian National University, Canberra

Alexander Motyl, Rutgers University-Newark, USA

Vlad Mykhnenko, University of Oxford, United Kingdom

Vitalii Ogiienko, Ukrainian Institute of National Remembrance, Kyiv

Olga Onuch, University of Manchester, United Kingdom

Olesya Ostrovska, Museum "Mystetskyi Arsenal," Kyiv

Anna Osypchuk, National University of Kyiv-Mohyla Academy

Oleksandr Pankieiev, University of Alberta, Edmonton

Oleksiy Panych, Publishing House "Dukh i Litera," Kyiv

Valerii Pekar, Kyiv-Mohyla Business School, Ukraine

Yohanan Petrovsky-Shtern, Northwestern University, Chicago

Serhii Plokhy, Harvard University, Cambridge, USA

Andrii Portnov, Viadrina University, Frankfurt-Oder, Germany

Maryna Rabinovych, Kyiv School of Economics, Ukraine

Valentyna Romanova, Institute of Developing Economies, Tokyo

Natalya Ryabinska, Collegium Civitas, Warsaw, Poland

Darya Tsymbalyk, University of Oxford, United Kingdom

Vsevolod Samokhvalov, University of Liege, Belgium

Orest Semotiuk, Franko National University, Lviv

Viktoriya Sereda, NAS Institute of Ethnology, Lviv

Anton Shekhovtsov, University of Vienna, Austria

Andriy Shevchenko, Media Center Ukraine, Kyiv

Oxana Shevel, Tufts University, Medford, USA

Pavlo Shopin, National Pedagogical Dragomanov University, Kyiv

Karina Shyrokykh, Stockholm University, Sweden

Nadja Simon, freelance interpreter, Cologne, Germany

Olena Snigova, NAS Institute for Economics and Forecasting, Kyiv

Ilona Solohub, Analytical Platform "VoxUkraine," Kyiv

Iryna Solonenko, LibMod - Center for Liberal Modernity, Berlin

Galyna Solovei, National University of Kyiv-Mohyla Academy

Sergiy Stelmakh, NAS Institute of World History, Kyiv

Olena Stiazhkina, NAS Institute of the History of Ukraine, Kyiv

Dmitri Stratievski, Osteuropa Zentrum (OEZB), Berlin

Dmytro Stus, National Taras Shevchenko Museum, Kyiv

Frank Sysyn, University of Toronto, Canada

Olha Tokariuk, Center for European Policy Analysis, Washington

Olena Tregub, Independent Anti-Corruption Commission, Kyiv

Hlib Vyshlinsky, Centre for Economic Strategy, Kyiv

Mychailo Wynnyckyj, National University of Kyiv-Mohyla Academy

Yelyzaveta Yasko, NGO "Yellow Blue Strategy," Kyiv

Serhy Yekelchyk, University of Victoria, Canada

Victor Yushchenko, President of Ukraine 2005-2010, Kyiv

Oleksandr Zaitsev, Ukrainian Catholic University, Lviv

Kateryna Zarembo, National University of Kyiv-Mohyla Academy

Yaroslav Zhalilo, National Institute for Strategic Studies, Kyiv

Sergei Zhuk, Ball State University at Muncie, USA

Alina Zubkovych, Nordic Ukraine Forum, Stockholm

Liudmyla Zubrytska, National University of Kyiv-Mohyla Academy